Praise for

His Brain, Her Brain

We felt like the Larimores were in our living room listening to us when we read *His Brain, Her Brain*. What an awesome book! No other book targets divine design in men and women like this book. Together Walt and Barb hit a bull's-eye on why men and women are so completely different; yet it is the differences that strengthen the marital union!

GARY ROSBERG, EdD, and BARB ROSBERG, BFA,
cofounders of America's Family Coaches,
authors of *The Five Sex Needs of Men and Women*

Walt Larimore has always been a trusted voice providing sound advice and compassionate insight. Now he teams up with a fabulous woman, his wife, Barb, to write a fascinating book about how incredibly we are designed. I loved *His Brain, Her Brain*. Every page offered an "aha" moment for me. I've definitely found a new wedding and anniversary gift I can give with confidence! Thanks, Walt and Barb.

JENNIFER ROTHSCHILD,
author, *Self Talk, Soul Talk*

We are different by God's design. The bad news is that the differences we don't understand often lead to division. The good news is that those same differences, in God's hands, can lead from dissonance and division to a rich and rewarding harmony. Walt and Barb have given us the gift of a handbook of help and hope that will both encourage us and provide us with simple and practical ways to enjoy a deeper, more meaningful, more intimate love relationship. This is a book you'll want to share with your friends.

Gary J. Oliver, PhD, executive director,
The Center for Relationship Enrichment
at John Brown University

The missing pieces we've all looked for in a marriage come together in *His Brain, Her Brain*! Walt and Barb do an amazing job of pulling out the differences in our makeup as men and women and turning them into unifying factors. Every couple in America should grab a copy of this book if they truly want a fulfilling, lifelong marriage. It's more than just a "gender difference book"; it's an eye-opener and marriage saver!

Joe White, EdD,
president of Kanakuk Kamps

Walt and Barb Larimore have written an engaging, practical manual that will make you laugh and think and will encourage the transformation that allows you to become the husband or wife God designed you to be. Cutting-edge medical science. Solid biblical truth. Practical marital wisdom. A genuine gem for the married and for those seeking a mate.

WILLIAM R. CUTRER, MD,
Gheens professor of Christian ministry,
The Southern Baptist Theological Seminary

———

Powerful, perceptive, and practical. *His Brain, Her Brain* is a miracle medication for marriages. It clears the fog that causes relationship collisions. Don't drive home without it.

DAVID STEVENS, MD, MA (Ethics),
chief executive officer,
Christian Medical & Dental Associations

———

Dr. Walt and Barb Larimore's book has opened my eyes even further to the truth about how wonderfully different men and women are. They give new insights and mind-expanding information about women for all of us to marvel with honor at how God has created them so special.

GARY SMALLEY, PhD,
author of *Change Your Heart,
Change Your Life*

A delightful, insightful, and important read for every couple —and for those who counsel and minister to them.

TIM CLINTON, EdD,
president, American Association
of Christian Counselors

Barb and Walt Larimore beautifully blend humor and easy-to-understand neuroscience to reveal the mysteries of how women and men are uniquely wired. These discoveries are certain to rescue many marriages and bring fulfillment to many more. I wish I had read *His Brain, Her Brain* early in my marriage. I plan to give a copy to each of my children and their spouses.

GENE RUDD, MD, senior vice president,
Christian Medical & Dental Associations

Judy and I have been married for forty-three years and have found *His Brain, Her Brain* to be very helpful in thinking through our relationship as it exists now and where it could go in the future. Thanks to Walt and Barb for writing a very practical, straightforward book to help couples who desire to honor God with their marriages.

RON BLUE, MBA,
president of Christian Financial
Professionals Network

The Larimores have written a wonderful book that makes the perfect wedding gift! Many of us have tried for decades to figure out our spouses. The Larimores have unraveled the mystery of male and female in a way that is not only an enjoyable read, but educational as well. So what are you waiting for? Pick up a copy of this book, and begin to surprise your spouse with all of your newfound understanding!

DIANE PASSNO,
senior vice president,
Focus on the Family

Do you want a better "brain"? Or put another way, do you want better *relationships* by understanding how Almighty God wired our brains? If your answer is yes (and it should be if you're serious about building a strong family), then do what my wife and I did: *Read this book!* You won't find "over your head" technical here—just wise words from a couple smart enough to help you and me realize how fearfully and wonderfully we're made for great relationships!

JOHN TRENT, Ph.D.,
president, The Center for StrongFamilies,
author of *The Blessing*

My wife, Mary, and I absolutely love this book. We agree that if all engaged and married couples read this book with open minds and hearts, the divorce rate will drop significantly.

LYLE W. DORSETT, PhD,
Billy Graham professor of evangelism,
Beeson Divinity School

If you and your spouse want to better understand God's plan for marriage, learn how to identify God's blueprint for each of you, and use this knowledge to build a lasting and fulfilling marriage, *His Brain, Her Brain* may be just the tool the two of you need.

Don Hawkins, DMin,
president of Southeastern Bible College

———

Walt and Barb expertly blend humor, wise biblical counsel, and recent medical findings that prove men and women are hardwired differently. If you've ever wondered why you and your spouse keep having the same issues over and over, Walt and Barb not only help you appreciate your differences but also help your marriage *thrive* because of them. Is another book on marriage necessary? This one is. In fact, if you are going to buy only one book about marriage, this should be the one!

Kent C. Shih, MD, MAR,
author of *Preparing for a Career in Medicine*

———

Viva la difference! Walt and Barb document what we all know to be true from personal experience, then help us apply these wonderful God-created differences as husbands and wives.

Gary DeSalvo, ThM,
senior pastor, Temple Bible Church,
Temple, Texas

My wife, Norma, and I read *His Brain, Her Brain* together. Our friends Walt and Barb Larimore identify the physiological and chemical differences in men and women that explain so much about why men act the way they act and why women are the way they are. Norma and I immediately saw ourselves and our God-created differences in a new light. I wish we had read it thirty years ago!

WAYNE PEDERSON,
vice president of broadcasting,
Moody Bible Institute

—

I wasn't sure another book on men and women was needed. However, once I got into the meat of Walt and Barb's book, I began to feel differently. *His Brain, Her Brain* is an honest and accurate picture of men and women and the wonderful design God has in store for us. I loved the blend of clinical and practical. This is a book I will recommend to others.

DAVE FLOWER,
elder, Little Log Church,
Palmer Lake, Colorado

—

In *His Brain, Her Brain*, Walt and Barb Larimore will guide you into a much greater appreciation of the wonderful ways in which God has designed a husband and a wife to beautifully complement one another. I believe this excellent book will be used by the Lord to move many married men and women to a greater enjoyment of their oneness in Christ!

RODNEY WOOD, PhD,
president of The Mission Foundation

Other Resources by Walt Larimore, MD

Alternative Medicine: The Christian Handbook
(coauthored with Dónal O'Mathúna)

Best of Bryson City audio

*Bryson City Tales: Stories of a Doctor's First Year
of Practice in the Smoky Mountains*

*Bryson City Seasons: More Tales of a Doctor's Practice
in the Smoky Mountains*

*Bryson City Secrets: Even More Tales of a Small-Town Doctor
in the Smoky Mountains*

God's Design for the Highly Healthy Child
(with Stephen and Amanda Sorenson)

God's Design for the Highly Healthy Person (with Traci Mullins)

God's Design for the Highly Healthy Teen (with Mike Yorkey)

Going Public with Your Faith: Becoming a Spiritual Influence at Work
(coauthored with William Carr Peel)

Going Public with Your Faith: Becoming a Spiritual Influence at Work audio
(coauthored with William Carr Peel)

*Going Public with Your Faith: Becoming a Spiritual Influence
at Work — Groupware™ curriculum with video, DVD,
leader's guide, and participant's workbook*
(coauthored with William Carr Peel, with Stephen and Amanda Sorenson)

*The Honeymoon of Your Dreams: A Practical Guide to Planning
a Romantic Honeymoon* (coauthored with Susan A. Crockett)

Lintball Leo's Not-So-Stupid Questions about Your Body
(with John Riddle, illustrated by Mike Phillips)

*The Saline Solution: Becoming a Spiritual Influence in Your Medical
Practice, small-group curriculum with video, leader's guide,
and participant's workbook* (coauthored with William Carr Peel)

SuperSized Kids: How to Rescue Your Child from the Obesity Threat
(coauthored with Cheryl Flynt and Steve Halliday)

Why ADHD Doesn't Mean Disaster
(coauthored with Dennis Swanberg and Diane Passno)

His Brain, Her Brain

How *Divinely* Designed *Differences* Can *Strengthen* Your *Marriage*

Walt Larimore, MD
& Barb Larimore

■ ZONDERVAN®

ZONDERVAN.com/
AUTHORTRACKER
follow your favorite authors

ZONDERVAN®

His Brain, Her Brain
Copyright © 2008 by Walt Larimore

Requests for information should be addressed to:
Zondervan, *Grand Rapids, Michigan 49530*

Library of Congress Cataloging-in-Publication Data

Larimore, Walter L.
    His brain, her brain : how divinely designed differences can strengthen your marriage / Walt Larimore and Barb Larimore.
        p. cm.
    Includes bibliographical references and index.
    ISBN-10: 0-310-24028-X
    ISBN-13: 978-0-310-24028-0
       1. Marriage—Religious aspects—Christianity. 2. Brain—Sex differences. 3. Sex differences—Religious aspects—Christianity. 4. Human behavior—Physiological aspects. I. Larimore, Barb. II. Title.
    BV835.L3525 2007
    248.8′44—dc22
                                        2007029334

Interior design by Beth Shagene

Printed in the United States of America

09 10 11 12 13 • 22 21 20 19 18 17 16 15 14 13 12 11 10 9 8 7 6 5

To our parents,
Stan and Inez Shaw and Philip and Maxine Larimore,
who demonstrated lifelong devotion
and commitment to each other
during the good times and the hard times

———

To Bill and Jane Judge,
who have been our marriage mentors, example,
and dear friends for over twenty years

Contents

PART 1

His Brain, *Her Brain*
THE SCIENCE

PART 2

His Brain, *Her Brain*
THE DIFFERENCES

PART 3

His Brain, *Her Brain*
THE IMPACT ON RELATIONSHIPS

PART 4

His Brain, *Her Brain*
THE BEAUTY OF GOD'S DESIGN

Foreword

THOUSANDS OF YEARS AGO, THE COUPLES WE READ ABOUT IN THE BIBLE probably faced the same basic relationship puzzles we face today. I suspect that Sarah exasperatedly asked her girlfriends, "Why won't Abraham just *tell* me what he's feeling?" And he in turn asked the men in the next tent, "Why can't she just let things go?" Their daughter-in-law Rebekah probably exclaimed to Isaac, "I don't want you to *fix* it; I just want you to listen!" And it's just as probable that Isaac walked away muttering, "Well, it would help if you wouldn't go on and on for so long!"

Moses and Zipporah probably argued about Moses' stopping and asking for directions while wandering in the desert. And King David knew perfectly well that if he didn't look away the moment he saw Bathsheba up on that roof, there would be trouble.

You get the idea. So many relationship conundrums are not only universal; they are also timeless. They have little to do with circumstances or culture and everything to do with how our brains are wired.

The last ten years have brought an explosion of understanding in the field of brain science, with scientists completely revising their previous assumptions. By far the most important revelation is that brains are not unisex. Far, far from it. Instead, each of us has been created with either a specifically male brain or a specifically female brain; which affects everything—from how we process our innermost feelings (girls: fast; guys: slow) to how quickly our bodies can get ready for physical intimacy (um—take a wild guess).

As many readers know, I've spent the last few years investigating the key surprises we tend not to "get" about those who are most important to us—especially the things women need to know about men and vice versa. Although this process has been fascinating, it has also often been frustrating because, although I could say (for example), "This *is* how men usually think and feel" on a given subject, I had no answer to *why*.

Thankfully, in many cases, brain science explains why. And once we understand that there is a *physical* explanation behind so many confusing behaviors, it changes everything. For example, during a conflict, instead of a wife thinking, "He's just *choosing* to not share what he's feeling," she can realize that her husband's brain circuits are being overloaded by emotion, and it will probably take several hours before he is physically able to process or share his thoughts. Or a husband can realize that his wife's relative lack of testosterone means she physically *can't* warm up as quickly as he can sexually, and therefore needs to be approached differently.

Once I heard about the advances in brain science, I knew that getting a handle on it simply *had* to be the next step in my own research. But I confess I have put it off for more than a year just because I got a sinking feeling in my stomach every time I looked at the stack of unread research papers, journal publications, and textbook-type tomes sitting on the shelf by my desk.

Most of us simply *can't* plow through all the dense brain science research to mine the key nuggets that affect us every day. This is where *His Brain, Her Brain* comes in. I can't even describe how delighted I was when I saw that a couple who was respected both in medicine and ministry had tackled the reams of research so the rest of us don't have to. Walt and Barb Larimore have taken all the complicated brain science and pulled out the most important points we simply *have* to understand about each other, and then put it into terms we can understand. I devoured the material and instantly saw everywhere applications for my own marriage. I know you will, too.

So grab a snack and a drink, and get yourself settled in a comfortable chair because if you're anything like me, you'll find it really hard to stop reading.

Here's to celebrating the differences!

SHAUNTI FELDHAHN,
public speaker, syndicated
columnist, and bestselling
author of *For Women Only*,
and the companion book,
For Men Only

Acknowledgments

M<small>ANY PEOPLE HAVE CONTRIBUTED TO THIS BOOK.</small> W<small>E ARE DEEPLY</small> indebted to Zondervan for their support. Cindy Hays Lambert, while at Zondervan, had the vision for this book in its earliest stages. Sandy Vander Zicht has been our editor and champion during the development and publishing of the book. Sandy's expert guidance and coaching have been critical to us in developing, writing, and editing this book. Dirk Buursma, as usual, has pulled the final manuscript together beautifully. We are appreciative of his professional and prudent editing suggestions and skills that kept many errors from appearing in these pages. However, for any remaining mistakes, we take full credit.

Thanks to Scott Heagle and Karen Campbell for providing marketing and public relations expertise, to Beth Shagene for her superb interior design, and to Jeff Gifford for his fabulous cover design. Many others at Zondervan contributed to the final book, and we are thankful for them all.

During the development and writing of the manuscript, we were delighted to be able to work with our close friends and colleagues Stephen and Amanda Sorenson, who served as our developmental editors. Amanda became our main encourager, equipper, and editor during the development of this book. She has also been our confidante, cheerleader, and critic. Her amazing ability to weave words and the threads of our thoughts into a beautiful manuscript has been a valued gift. Thanks, Amanda, for your hand-holding, encouragement, and prayers during the final phases of writing this book.

Thanks to Paul Batura for research and permissions assistance and to Ned McLeod, our longtime business counsel and friend. We appreciate the design advice and expertise of Sally Dunn.

Many thanks go to those who took time to carefully review early drafts of the manuscript and offer suggestions that have improved the finished book—including Zanese Duncan; Gene Rudd, MD; Kent Shih, MD; David Stevens, MD; Pastor Chris Taylor; and Dr. Rodney Wood. We're also thankful to the elder board at our home church, the Little Log Church in Palmer Lake, Colorado (Pastor Bill Story, Jeff Ball, Dave Flower, and Rick Fisher) for their review and counsel. Thanks also to Allan Harmer, ThM, for his encouragement and affirmation.

Finally, and most important, we are grateful to God for allowing us to serve him through writing. Our deepest prayer is that this book will bring glory to him.

WALT AND BARB LARIMORE
Monument, Colorado
October 2007

Introduction

DOES THE WORLD REALLY NEED ANOTHER BOOK ABOUT MARRIAGE? NOT really. There are literally hundreds of such books, and many of them are best sellers. So I (Walt) wasn't interested in adding to that pile.

But I (Barb) did believe that there was a need for a book that would show what we women have always known—that our female brains are unique and that we think, feel, perceive, react, respond, love, need, and appreciate life and relationships differently from the way that our husbands do.

Barb was right. When we began to understand how God designed us to be very different, and yet to be his gifts to each other, we began to experience a more fulfilling and meaningful marriage. And so we began to talk about writing a book that would help other men and women discover how their differences could lead to more satisfying and significant marriages for them as well.

By understanding how God created and designed us, we are more likely to turn our myriad differences, blind spots, and weaknesses into oneness and strength, so that we can more fully live the joy of God's delightful design for marriage.

If the concept that his brain and her brain are different from the womb is new to you, rest assured that the idea was once new to me also. It wasn't until after college and medical school that I finally became convinced.

It's no wonder it took Walt so long. He grew up with no sisters. However, my sister and I have brothers, so we knew that boys and girls were different, even before we had the vocabulary to say so.

OK, I admit I was a bit dense about this. During my adolescent and college years, I bought into the popular arguments that men and women were basically the same and that we only became different under the influence of culture, environment, nurture, and society. Then several events changed my tune.

First, I fell in love with Barb when we were high school seniors, and I had to begin to learn firsthand the many differences between our brains.

Second, during college, Barb and I began to study the Bible together. Among the many things we learned was that God had created men and women to be uniquely different. Not only that, these divinely inspired differences were designed to strengthen our relationship with God and each other.

When we read the Bible together, we found astounding insight and wisdom into how men and women could be transformed by God's principles and by a personal relationship with him into better people, better spouses, and better parents—not to mention building a better marriage by understanding our divinely devised differences.

Third, during my years in medical practice, I became aware of the findings of dozens of scientists who had begun to discover innumerable innate differences between the brains of men and women. I was particularly impressed by some of the dynamic and dramatic differences between male and female brains and brain chemicals.

We searched through scores of studies, books, and websites to bring to you the most up-to-date and practical findings from scientific researchers around the world. As Barb and I discussed these findings, we were amazed at the science of why men and women think and act the way we do.

What's even more amazing, these differences not only made sense to us from a scientific viewpoint, but we realized we were living them! These divinely designed differences affect how we think, react, respond, and behave every day.

Each of the factors has supported the biblical teaching regarding the differences between men and women. What the scientists have found correlates with what we've discovered about the Creator's blueprint for husbands and wives. When understood and applied according to biblical principles, we believe God-designed differences can make your marriage—as it did ours—more satisfying and stable.

As we bring you what we've learned, I (Barb) will work as hard as I can to keep Walt from diving too deeply into what I call "boring science." I often have to remind him to avoid giving out TMI—too much information. And while I had a hand in every part of this book, for the sake of simplicity Walt will be the main narrator. When I need to say something from my viewpoint alone, you'll find the words in italics, just like this, so you can readily identify who is talking.

Barb and I agreed that we wanted you to have enough information to understand each other but also enough practical tips to apply this information effectively to your marriage and relationships. However, we provide plenty of citations at the back of our book so that those with a thirst for additional details can find more information on the research and applicable theology.

Although we believe our experience is typical and applicable to most men and women, we are going to be talking about a lot of generalities. So what we say may not apply 100 percent to you. Take what you need and leave the rest.

When we refer to men and women, or girls and boys, we will be referring to "most," and almost never "all." We realize there will be exceptions to what we say—perhaps even in *your* life and marriage. But we encourage you not to throw the baby out with the bathwater. Take note of the exceptions, but keep on reading and have fun learning.

Our aim is simple: to assist you in seeing the value of your spouse (or spouse-to-be) and his or her unique design and differences.

Our goal is to help you strengthen your marriage by helping men understand their wife's brain and assisting women to understand their husband's brain so that you and your spouse can serve God and others much more effectively than you ever could apart. When you become a person who loves and celebrates your and your spouse's divinely developed and delightful brain differences (*because* of the differences and not just *in spite* of them), then you will have a stronger foundation for lifelong love.

If we fail to understand and appreciate these Creator-conceived brain differences as gifts and strengths, then we may find ourselves echoing the thoughts of Katharine Hepburn: "Sometimes I wonder if men and women really suit each other. Perhaps they should live next door and just visit now and then."[1]

We pray that this book will be a tremendous encouragement and a fun read for you and your spouse. It is our fondest hope that God will use his principles and his Word to teach and stimulate you to understand and approach your spouse as the specially created and unique gift that he or she is intended to be.

As you read this book, as you meditate on its principles, and as you compare its content to the Bible, expect to see the Creator of his brain and her brain begin to work in *your* brain and mind and heart. As you apply the suggestions in this book and as you consider how to implement them in your life, expect to see your marriage begin to change.

So be ready to be surprised. Expect to laugh. Most of all, be ready to put these principles to work—for your sake, your marriage's sake, for the sake of your children if you're blessed with them, and for the sake of God's glory.

PART 1

His Brain,

The Science

1

Chapter

Different by Divine Design

Our good friend Chris came over to our home one Saturday morning to share some time together over a cup of coffee. Chris and his wife, Sherri, had been married for about six months. They had chosen Barb and me to be their marriage mentors, so we had met with them during their engagement and continued to do so after the wedding. After discussing our observations of the Denver Broncos' football season, Chris and I began talking about marriage.

"Walt," he began, "when Sherri and I met with you and Barb before we were married, you taught us about some of the differences between men and women and our brains. I accepted what you said but didn't realize exactly how big a deal it really is."

"In what ways?" I asked.

"I don't even know where to begin. There are *so* many ways we are different. When it comes to sex, Sherri likes thirty minutes of slow foreplay. For me, turning off our bedroom light is foreplay. I like watching football and *The Unit*, and she likes watching *Dancing with the Stars* and anything on HGTV."

While he took a sip of coffee, I remained quiet, knowing more was coming.

"When I write a note to Sherri, it has the essentials—what she needs to know. When Sherri writes me a note, she uses scented, colored stationery and dots her *i*'s with little hearts. Even if she disses me in a note, she puts a dorky little smiley face at the end. I *hate* that! What's worse, she wants me to write notes the same way."

He appeared to be deep in thought and then continued.

"Here's another thing that bugs me. When I say I'm ready to leave the house, it means I'm ready to leave at that moment. When Sherri says she is ready to go, it means she will be ready sometime in the next hour—after she finishes her hair and makeup and changing her outfit two or three times.

"And don't get me started on the bathroom," Chris added. "I have, at most, six items in the bathroom—shaving cream, a razor, a toothbrush, toothpaste, a bar of soap, and deodorant. But Sherri must have sixty items! I don't even know what fifty of them are for.

"And, Walt, isn't a cell phone a communications tool? I use mine to communicate information in short calls and brief text messages or to get an answer. Sherri uses her cell phone to visit with a girlfriend for two hours *after* they've had lunch that same day!"

He finally stopped, and I was able to get a word in. "So, Chris, what does all this mean to you?"

He thoughtfully sipped his coffee and then nodded. "You were right when you told me that men and women are *so* different. Now I've got to figure out what to do about it."

We Do See It Differently!

The story has been told of an English professor who wrote on a blackboard these words:

A woman without her man is nothing

The professor then directed the students to punctuate the phrase. Most of the men wrote:

A woman, without her man, is nothing.

However, most of the women recorded:

A woman: without her, man is nothing![1]

It's Not Just Our Imagination

Chris is absolutely correct. Even without scientific evidence, the vast majority of us realize that men and women are *very* different. One online poll asked simply if people agreed with the statement "Men and women are so different." Seventy percent clicked the "Yes, worlds apart!" answer. Eighteen percent chose "Not really. It's all hype." And 12 percent selected "I'm never sure."[2]

My friends will talk about how their husbands are sometimes thoughtless or inconsiderate, don't listen like they should, think too much about sex and sports, aren't as compassionate as they could be, want to have sex rather than make love, and don't put the toilet seat down as they should.

From the other side, I often hear my male friends complain about the way their wives drive, that they can't read maps right-side-up, talk and cry too much, can't explain their intuitive feelings, don't initiate sex often enough, and leave the toilet seat down when it clearly should be left up.

In their book *Why Men Don't Listen and Women Can't Read Maps*, authors Barbara and Allan Pease make this observation:

> Men can never find a pair of socks, but their CDs are in alphabetical order. Women can always find the missing set of car keys but rarely the most direct route to their destination. Men marvel at the way a woman can walk into a room full of people and give an instant commentary on everyone; women can't believe men are so unobservant.[3]

These differences are not something we imagine. They are not volitional choices we make just to annoy each other. They are not simply due to personality quirks. Many, if not most, of these dissimilarities have to do with the distinctive ways his brain and her brain function.

A mountain of brain research published during the last two decades reveals dramatic anatomical, chemical, hormonal, and physiological differences between his brain and her brain. These differences impact the emotions, thinking, and behavior of children and adults. These differences are so profound that geneticist Anne Moir, PhD, and journalist David Jessel begin their book *Brain Sex: The Real Difference Between Men and Women* with this provocative assertion: "Men are different from women. They are equal only in their common membership in the same species, humankind. To maintain that they are the same in aptitude, skill or behavior is to build a society based on a biological and scientific lie."[4]

Our Differences: Wired in the Womb

So, if his brain and her brain are so very different, are these differences inborn or infused? Are men's and women's brains different by nature or nurture? Are our brain differences designed or derived?

Our answer to these questions is simple: not only are his brain and her brain different; they are *designed* to be different by our Creator. At birth, his brain and her brain are so distinctly different that Cambridge University neuropsychologist Simon Baron-Cohen, PhD, describes them as having "essential differences."[5]

There is ample scientific evidence that supports the fact that many of the dramatic differences between his brain and her brain are inborn. Louann Brizendine, MD, a neuropsychiatrist at the University of California, San Francisco, medical school, writes, "There is no unisex brain. Girls arrive already wired as girls, and boys arrive already wired as boys. Their brains are different by the time they're born."[6]

In surprisingly frank language, Dr. Anne Moir writes, "Infants are not blank slates.... They are born with male or female minds of their own. They have, quite literally, made up their minds in the womb, safe from the legions of social engineers who impatiently await them."[7]

Our only quibble with Dr. Moir's conclusion is that unborn children do not make up their minds in the womb. Rather, an unborn child's brain and nervous system is intentionally and skillfully interwoven and knit in the womb. Or as King David observed:

> *You [God] created my inmost being;*
> *you knit me together in my mother's womb.*
> *I praise you because I am fearfully and wonderfully made;*
> *your works are wonderful,*
> *I know that full well.*
> *My frame was not hidden from you when I was made in the*
> *secret place.*
> *When I was woven together in the depths of the earth,*
> *your eyes saw my unformed body.*[8]

As we'll discover together, plenty of differences are seen extremely early in development—even in the womb. And every mom reading this book who has raised a boy and a girl has observed these differences firsthand! Although some researchers persist in the assertion that the many differences we all observe between males and females are a result of "nurture over nature" (nurture meaning differences based on culture, socialization, teaching, or experience), there is one event that can shake this delusion to its core, namely, having children.

Marc Breedlove, PhD, an expert in the effect of hormones on the developing brain, was also a proponent of the "nurture over nature" theory—at least until he had a daughter. He was surprised that she had no interest in her older brothers' toys. He was shocked that even before she could talk she loved going into her mother's closet to try on her mother's shoes. By the time she was six years old, Breedlove's daughter avoided pants and would only wear dresses. As a result, Breedlove "uses the term 'childless' to describe people who think 'society alone molds children into sex roles.'"[9]

Testosterone on the Brain

So what do we know about the processes in the womb that prewire girls to be girls and boys to be boys? During the past couple of decades, we've learned more than you would ever imagine, and it all begins with the male hormone, testosterone.

We've all heard the jokes about female hormones. We know how dramatically they affect women. We've all seen men roll their eyes, shake their heads, and mutter "female hormones" when life with a woman seems difficult. But let me tell you, what female hormones do to women is minor compared to what the male hormone, testosterone, does to an unborn boy's brain and body in the womb!

At about six weeks' gestation, an unborn boy's male hormones (called *androgens*) begin their work. One particular androgen, testosterone, becomes the key messenger to the unborn boy's brain and body. "There's a peak of testosterone in males ... that's very important for future sexual behavior," writes Dr. Sophie Messager of Paradigm Therapeutics in Cambridge, England. "If you block that, the male rats behave like females for the rest of their life."[10]

Testosterone tells all the potentially female equipment to go into hibernation while it spurs the male equipment (like the boy's genitalia) to grow like crazy. In addition, testosterone has an incredible effect on the little boy's skeletal muscles—causing them to almost continuously twitch, poke, and punch.

Those of us who have given birth to and then raised little boys can tell you that they are always *moving, both in and out of the womb! Much of the activity is due to testosterone, which also thickens the boy's developing bones—even his skull. So when we mothers think little boys and the men they grow up to become seem a bit "hardheaded," we're exactly right.*

Not only are a boy's genitalia, muscles, and bones dramatically exposed to the testosterone bath that occurs in the womb, but it actually changes his inborn female brain into a uniquely male brain.[11] The developing female brain, not exposed to testosterone, undergoes very little fundamental change in structure or function, but the rush of testosterone is for him literally a mind-altering process!

For example, the corpus callosum is the largest structure connecting the right and left sides of the brain. This pipeline of more than 300 million fibers[12] functions like a powerful, lightning-fast monster cable that enables both sides of the brain to communicate with and process for each other. The gush of testosterone actually causes sections of the corpus callosum to decrease in size by dissolving portions of the connection or by decreasing the growth of the nerves.[13]

In unborn females, the opposite happens. Exposure to the female hormone, estrogen, actually prompts the nerve cells to grow more connections between the left and right brain. So not only is a girl's corpus callosum larger than a boy's before birth, it continues to be larger in childhood[14] and adulthood.[15]

Testosterone also causes other areas of the male brain to be forever changed by preserving the nerve cells that think, while retarding the development of the fibers that connect the processing centers. The result? Your wife not only has a more developed corpus callosum, but she also has much greater subconscious processing power than you do.

It's More Than Hormones

The male hormones flooding in and through the unborn male child and the female hormones saturating the unborn female baby do not explain everything about the developmental differences between the male and female brain. There are structural and genetic differences as well.

Since a man's brain is, on average, about 10 percent larger than a woman's, you'd expect him to be more intelligent. However, this is not the case. In general, men and women consistently score equally on intelligence tests. For neuroscientists, this has long been a paradox. However, researchers at the University of Pennsylvania Medical Center have found an explanation. Raquel E. Gur, MD, PhD, professor of psychiatry and neurology, writes, "Women's brains appear to be more efficient than men's in the sense that an equal increase in volume produces a larger increase in processing capacity in women than in men."[16]

While male brains contain about 6.5 times more gray matter —the "thinking matter"—female brains have more than 9.5 times as much white matter—the "processing matter."[17] One example is seen in the corpus callosum. Not only do women have a relatively larger connection between the hemispheres, but theirs is composed almost completely of white matter. "The implication of women having more white matter connecting between the hemispheres of the brain is that they would have better communication between the different modes of perceiving and relating to the world," says Dr. Gur. "On the other hand, men," who have a relatively smaller corpus callosum that is made up of less white matter, "would demonstrate a stronger concentration on working within any one of those modes."[18]

Understanding this can be critical in understanding our husbands —their stick-to-itiveness, steadfastness, determination, and single-mindedness. It also can assist their understanding and appreciation of us—our intuition and the way we can read people!

On the genetic side, Eric Vilain, PhD, who conducts research on the genetics of human sexual development at UCLA, has found genetic differences that play a role in the disparity between the male and female brain. He and his colleagues compared the production of genes in male and female brains in embryonic mice—long before the animals developed sex organs.[19] To their surprise, the researchers found at least fifty-four genes that are produced in different amounts in male and female mouse brains *prior to* any male hormonal influence. Eighteen of these genes were found at higher levels in the male brains, while thirty-six were found at higher levels in the female brains.

"We didn't expect to find genetic differences between the sexes' brains," Dr. Vilain said in a news interview. "But we discovered that the male and female brains differed in many measurable ways, including anatomy and function."[20] Although this study was in mice, these researchers believe it's highly likely to be true in people as well.

Additional studies show that "sex chromosome genes contribute directly to the development of a sex difference in the brain."[21] To understand this impact, we need to review some sex chromosome basics.

At conception, one pair of sex chromosomes* is replicated into each cell of our body; one comes from each parent. As a general rule, males have one X and one Y chromosome and females have two X chromosomes. As a little boy begins to grow inside the womb, his genetic blueprint begins to deliver a message using his XY chromosomes. Little girls do the same but with XX chromosomes.

Many of the genes on the Y chromosome are involved in male differentiation and development. It is the male-making Y chromosome that starts the marathon of development that differentiates the little boy and his brain from the little girl and her brain. The Y chromosome directs the early gonadal tissue of the boy to become testes—and it's the testes that are the primary factory for the production of testosterone that spurs the development of masculinity across the brain and body of the unborn boy.

A normal female has two X chromosomes—one from her mother and one from her father. One of the two X chromosomes in every cell in females is active, and the other X chromosome is usually shut off. Researchers have found that brain responses vary based on which X gene is inactivated.[22] About one in five of these

---

* A chromosome is a rod-shaped or threadlike DNA-containing structure located in the nucleus of each cell in the body.

extra genes escapes being turned off and actually stays awake. When this occurs, these female cells get a "double dose" of X genes. These excess or fallback genes are believed to help protect women from a wide variety of physical, mental, and behavioral disorders.[23]

These excess genes also result in more genetic diversity in the female brain. *New York Times* columnist Maureen Dowd wrote, "Women are not only more different from men than we knew. Women are more different from each other than we knew—creatures of 'infinite variety,' as Shakespeare wrote." Dowd concludes, "This means men's generalizations about women are correct too. Women are inscrutable, changeable, crafty, idiosyncratic, a different species."[24]

Regarding the advantages of two X chromosomes, Duke University genome expert Huntington Willard, PhD, says, "We poor men only have 45 chromosomes to do our work with because our 46th is the pathetic Y that has only a few genes.... In contrast, we now know that women have the full 46 chromosomes that they're getting work from and the 46th is a second X that is working at levels greater than we knew."[25]

> There is more to be known, more detail and qualification perhaps to add—but the nature and cause of brain differences are now known beyond speculation, beyond prejudice, and beyond reasonable doubt.[26]
>
> **Anne Moir, PhD**

Dr. Willard, along with Laura Carrel, PhD, a molecular biologist at the Pennsylvania State University College of Medicine, found that a whopping 15 percent (200-300) of the genes on the second X chromosome in women, thought to be inactive and silenced, are active, giving women significantly more gene activity than men.[27] The two X chromosomes in women are another part of the explanation of how the very different behavior and traits of men and women are hardwired in the brain, in addition to being hormonal or cultural.[28]

Divine Design

Since it is apparent that many of the differences between his brain and her brain are real and inborn, the next logical question is, "What is their origin?" Most published researchers on this topic seem to believe that the distinctions and dissimilarities between men's and women's brains are simply the divergences and diversity of evolution. We are convinced, however, that his brain and her brain are not only divinely designed to be delightfully different but are, in fact, deliberately designed differently. The foundation for our belief is found in the book of Genesis, where Moses writes this:

> Then God said, "Let us make man in our image, in our likeness, and let them rule over the fish of the sea and the birds of the air, over the livestock, over all the earth, and over all the creatures that move along the ground." So God created man in his own image, in the image of God he created him; male and female he created them. God blessed them and said to them, "Be fruitful and increase in number; fill the earth and subdue it. Rule over the fish of the sea and the birds of the air and over every living creature that moves on the ground."[29]

It seems clear from this passage that men and women were created equally in the image of God: "male and female he created *them*. God blessed *them*" (emphasis ours).[30] The biblical point of view is not that men are from Mars and women are from Venus. Rather, men and women were lovingly created on earth in the image of God. Thus, we carry in our innermost being the stamp of our Creator.

The Bible is also clear that "equal" is not synonymous with "the same." Men and women were created equal, but men and women were not created the same or in the same way. We were created different and differently — in other words, males and females are designed differently and designed to be different.*

Different from Day One

The genetic, hormonal, and created differences in his brain and her brain occur long before birth and any chance of socialization. The resulting differences can be seen in the womb, throughout infancy and childhood, and into our adult years.

For example, in the newborn nursery and in one-year-olds, girls consistently make more eye contact with adults than boys of the same age.[31] The differences become more obvious as children grow and develop. In preschool, when a new toy is brought to the playground, boys invariably leave whatever they are doing and go look it over. However, when new children come to the playground, the girls are more likely to go meet them than boys are.[32] Furthermore, when compared to boys, girls learn to speak earlier, know more words, recall them better, pause less, and glide through tongue twisters.[33]

Harriet Wehner Hanlon, PhD, and her associates at Virginia Tech University examined the brain activity of more than five hundred children aged two months to over sixteen years and concluded that the areas of the brain involved in language, spatial memory, motor coordination, and getting along with other people develop in a different order, time, and rate in girls compared with boys.[34]

These differences play out in a number of ways. For example, talking is central to the friendships of females at every age. Physician and psychologist Leonard Sax, MD, PhD, observes, "The mark of a truly close friendship between two girls or two women is that they tell each other secrets they don't tell anyone else."[35] On the other hand, boys don't spend a lot of time talking to each other,

---

* We will explain this concept in detail in chapter 13.

nor do they want to hear each other's secrets. They are much more likely to build models, operate toys, or play video games.[36]

Do these brain differences between the genders even out over time? Not usually. Females and males maintain unique brain characteristics throughout life. There are advantages and disadvantages to these differences. For example, females derive strength and consolation from intimate friendships and conversation. When girls and women are under stress, they'll often look to each other for support and comfort.[37] Not males. When boys and men are under stress, they usually want to do something physical or be left alone.[38]

Researchers are beginning to recognize that these differences are not bad but good. Ruben C. Gur, PhD, says, "Most of these differences are complementary. They increase the chances of males and females joining together. It helps the whole species."[39] To us, these differences also point to the way God designed and created us.

Walt and I observed many inborn differences between boys and girls as our children, Kate and Scott, grew up. We would dress Kate in her Sunday best, and she'd be just perfect when we arrived at church. Scott, dressed for the same event, could rarely make it to the car without finding a puddle to stomp in or a stick needing an adventure.

Scott's room was chronically malodorous and messy. Kate's room was occasionally messy but always smelled good.

With her dolls, Kate would play house and make up elaborate stories. Scott would take Kate's dolls and set them up to battle each other. Then he would tear off their heads, arms, or legs.

Kate began to think of her future mate at a very early age. At the same age, Scott thought girls had cooties and should never be touched.

At an even earlier age, Kate could talk in complete sentences. At the same age, Scott could only make the sounds of machine guns and bombs blowing up.

It was obvious to Barb and me that these differences between Kate and Scott were not a result of culture, environment, or socialization—not a result of how they were taught or what they saw modeled in our home. Our parents saw the same traits in us, and we still see them in each other.

I dress up in my Sunday best to go to church and will still be clean and unwrinkled when we arrive. But somehow, Walt rarely makes it through the garage without having to fiddle with something and seems to always pick up grease or dirt.

OK, I admit, my side of the closet is mildly messy and has the faint odor of wet socks—while Barb's side is orderly and always smells good. And if Barb accidentally burps (well, belches), she is embarrassed and always says, "Excuse me." I hardly notice when air or gas escapes—although Barb can pick this up across the room.

I still make more eye contact with my friends than Walt does. I like talking with my friends. Walt likes briefer and louder, more boisterous conversations with his friends. I like people—Walt likes projects.

Ah, we are different! And Barb and I have come not only to see but also to appreciate the differences between her brain and my brain. We see it as a part of a divine design—differences that are created and woven together before we ever take our first breath.

As we've shared with our friends Chris and Sherri what we've learned, they too have come to appreciate how very different his brain and her brain are designed to be. Now, instead of saying, "I've got to figure out what to do about these brain differences," Chris smiles and says, *"Vive la difference!"* Understanding these differences is resulting in a strengthening of their marriage of eight years. We believe it will help your marriage too.

2

Chapter

Different as Night and Day

WHENEVER I HAD THE OPPORTUNITY TO ASSIST IN BRAIN SURGERY ON one of my patients, I was there! I was fascinated by the brain and how amazingly intricate and complicated it is. However, once you look inside the skull, you simply cannot tell if a brain is male or female — at least not by looking. The differences, however, are huge and are based in large part on the circuitry and chemicals that our Creator wove together while we were still in the womb.

During my medical school training before CTs, MRIs, or PET scans,* the subject of neuroscience intrigued me. But I never considered knowledge of the brain to be a relationship and marriage tool. That was *not* on my radar screen — it wasn't even a thought that had crossed my mind.

However, the dramatic advances in brain study and imaging techniques over the last thirty years have made neuroscience even more fascinating than it was before. Using specialized functional imaging of the brain (i.e., fCT, fMRI and fPET scans),† which records the increased blood flow that accompanies certain neural

---

* All three are noninvasive imaging tests that can be used to peer painlessly through the skull and into the brain and produce two- or three-dimensional images. CT = computed tomography; MRI = magnetic resonance imaging; and PET = positron emission tomography.

† fCT = functional CT; fMRI = functional MRI; and fPET = functional PET.

activity, researchers can actually map mental activity. As a result, scientists are just beginning to understand the differences
between the male and female brain. And to help you understand
some of the basics of this new science and to recognize the impact
of these differences on relationships and marriages, I'll need to
introduce you to a few brain structures and chemicals.

*I'll let Walt share some of this scientific information with you,
but I promise to help him keep it simple! And I'll stay away from
demeaning jokes like, "Men have two brains — one's lost and
the other is out looking for it — and not asking for directions
to find it!" I simply will* not *resort to such sophomoric humor.
However, I think the neuroanatomy drawing in figure 1 is fairly
accurate — don't you?*

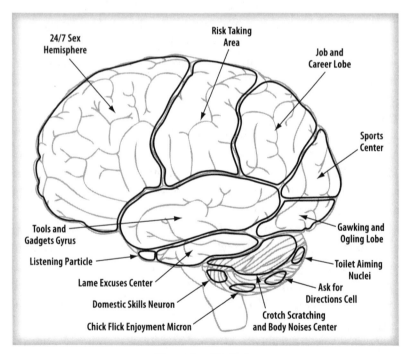

Figure 1 — His Brain

Well, turnaround is fair play, so let me show you figure 2, my illustration of the female brain.

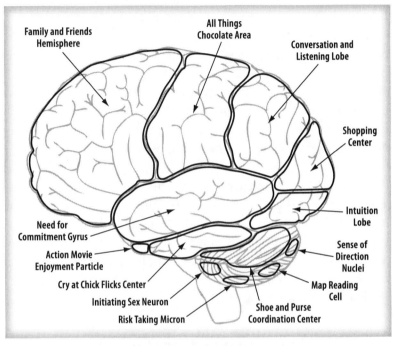

Figure 2 — Her Brain

Our daughter-in-law, Jennifer, who is a PhD candidate in neurobiology, helped us develop these illustrations for you, and we hope you enjoyed them. But if that's as much science as you can stand, then you may want to skim the rest of the chapter and look at the tables on pages 48, 50, and 55 that summarize the information Walt will share.

For those of you who are more inquisitive, let me introduce you to an absolutely wonderful creation — the human brain. The brain can process speech, complex visual images, and a wide spectrum of sound. It controls your body temperature, blood pressure, heart rate, and breathing. It accepts a flood of information about the world around you from your various senses. It handles physical motion when you walk, talk, stand, chew, swallow, or just sit. It lets you think, dream, reason, and experience emotions.

The average brain, weighing in at only about three pounds, or 2 percent of the average body's mass, uses 20 percent of the oxygen you breathe and 25 percent of the calories you eat. In addition, approximately 20 percent of the blood flowing from the heart is pumped to the brain.[1] It has 100 billion neurons—which is amazing when you consider that the entire Milky Way galaxy is said to contain roughly 100 billion planets and stars.

The brain needs constant blood flow, oxygen, and calories to keep up with the heavy metabolic demands[2] of its 100 trillion synapses or connections[3] that operate at lightning speed. In fact, the brain has been estimated to handle ten quadrillion instructions per second, which is ten times the theoretical maximum speed of the top supercomputer, which may handle up to one quadrillion operations per second.[4]

The brain is amazing indeed!

Brain Anatomy for Dummies

Structurally, we can think of the brain as having three major sections: two—the cerebral cortex and brain stem—can be seen from the exterior of the brain (see figure 3), and the third—the limbic system—is deep in the brain (see figure 4).

The **brain stem**, including the **cerebellum**, is located where the skull and neck are joined. It is the area that regulates functions such as breathing, cardiovascular function, and digestion. Even when the higher areas of the brain are destroyed (as can occur with a severe stroke or head injury), the brain stem will usually keep functioning. It appears that this area of the brain is fairly similar between males and females. But as we move up the brain, the differences become impressive.

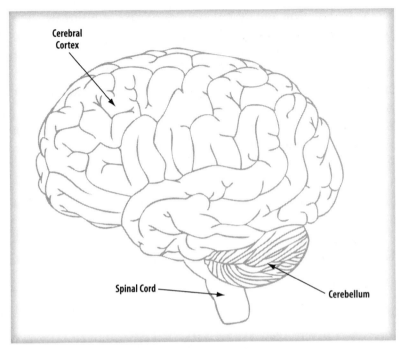

Figure 3 — Brain Sections

The **limbic system,** which is deep in the brain and wrapped around the brain stem, is designed to assist us in responding to sensory responses from the outside world. Every second, whether we are awake or asleep, the millions of sensory stimuli that come from the nerve endings of the skin, eyes, nose, ears, and taste buds (touch, vision, aroma, sound, taste) are processed by the limbic system.

When a stimulus is associated with an emotion for the first time, this "emotional memory" is imprinted in the limbic system. If a repeated stimulus sparks the emotional memory, then the limbic system passes it on to the upper and lower brain. Psychologist Turhan Canli, PhD, has shown that women encode memories using different and far more complex pathways than men use. As a result, women are better able to accurately recall a memory (compared to men) and the emotions and sensations that occurred when the memory was recorded.[5]

At least four major portions of the limbic system are different in males and females — the **hypothalamus**, the **amygdala**, the **hippocampus**, and the **cingulate gyrus**. The illustration in figure 4 shows the limbic system.

The **hypothalamus** is the brain's sex center. As you may imagine, this marble-sized gland is very different in his brain and her brain. It is highly sensitive to testosterone and is much larger in men than women. The size and sensitivity of this gland is part of the reason most men have much stronger sex drives than women.

The **hippocampus** and **amygdala** receive, process, and store emotional memory. The amygdala amplifies memories that are

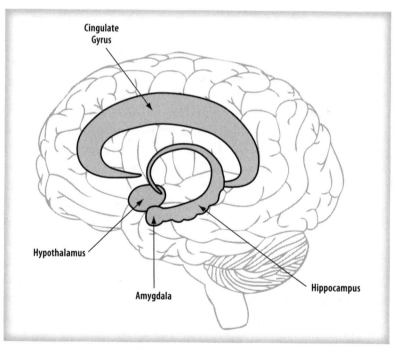

Figure 4 — Limbic System

pleasant or frightening. It communicates to the hippocampus which memories need to be locked in place and then strung together like pearls on a necklace. For example, it will never let you forget what you were doing on September 11, 2001.

These two areas of the limbic system are far larger and more active in women than in men, and they are far better connected in women than in men to the verbal and emotion handling centers of the brain. Therefore, women connect words and feelings to memories much more powerfully than men. As a result, men are far less likely to remember their emotional experiences. In men, these areas of the limbic system are far better connected to the spinal cord than they are to the cortex. Therefore, in responding to emotional stimuli, men are less likely and able to express feelings verbally and more inclined to respond physically.

The **cingulate gyrus** has been described as the "key emotion center in the limbic system."[6] Whereas emotion, intimacy, and bonding all have chemical and neural connections and conduction in and through the brain, the cingulate gyrus oversees this process. Not only is the cingulate gyrus larger and more active in women, it also has far more neural connections to the cerebral cortex than a man's (especially to the verbal and emotional processing areas on both sides of the cortex). This helps explain a woman's natural tendency to "tend and befriend," to nurture, and to talk about the feelings she experiences.

The **cerebral cortex** is the highest section of the brain (both in function and anatomically, when we are standing). The cerebral cortex is responsible for seeing, hearing, smelling, thinking, remembering, and reasoning. It also helps us with moral decision making, abstract thinking, designing, idealizing, making goals, finding motivation, and many other higher human functions.

These intricate connections between the body, limbic system, and the cerebral cortex—and the differences between how his brain and her brain makes these connections—is what impacts our relationships and marriages.

The cerebral cortex is divided into a left and right side, each called a hemisphere. Each hemisphere has distinct functions, as summarized in table 1.

Table 1 — Function of Each Hemisphere

Left Hemisphere	Right Hemisphere
Physically controls the right side of the body	Controls the left side of the body
The "rational" side of the brain	The creative and artistic side of the brain
Mentally deals with logic, reason, and speech	Mentally deals with ideas and imagination
Does specific analysis. Is the "practical" and "common sense" side of the brain	Does holistic thinking
Evaluates fine details	Evaluates the big picture
Processes linear thinking and specific tasks	Processes spatial thinking and multiprocessing
Remembers, for example, the words to a song	Remembers, for example, the tune of a song

In addition, each hemisphere of the brain is further divided into four lobes—the frontal, parietal, temporal, and occipital lobes. See figure 5.

The **frontal lobe** is primarily concerned with reasoning, planning, parts of speech, movement (motor cortex), emotions, and problem solving.

The **parietal lobe** is concerned with perception of stimuli related to touch, pressure, temperature, and pain.

The **temporal lobe** is concerned with perception and recognition of auditory stimuli (hearing) and memory.

The **occipital lobe** is located at the back of the brain and is concerned with many aspects of vision.

In addition, the cerebral cortex contains two types of matter or substance. **Gray matter** is where much of the brain's processing power and function occurs. **White matter** comprises the long fibers (axons) that transmit electrical signals around the brain and to and from the body.

Male brains have much more white matter connecting the thinking and reacting centers of the brain to the spinal cord than

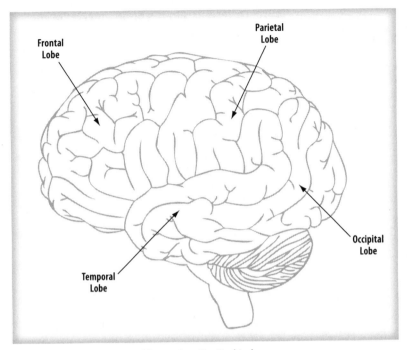

Figure 5 — Cortical Lobes

female brains. Therefore, men are designed for physical reactions over thinking reactions. Female brains have more white matter connecting the two hemispheres and are therefore better designed to multitask.

In later chapters we'll talk about the myriad ways in which these structural differences affect our marriages. But first let's use table 2 to summarize a few of the significant structural differences between his and her brain.

> *Male* and female brains are different in architecture and chemical composition. The sooner women — and those who love them — accept and appreciate how those neurological differences shape female behavior, the better we can all get along.[7]
>
> **Louann Brizendine, MD**

Table 2 — Structural Differences in His Brain and Her Brain

Brain Structure	His Brain	Her Brain
Corpus callosum	Smaller	Larger
Amygdala, hippocampus, and emotional memory	Smaller and less connected to the cerebral cortex but better connected to the spinal cord and body	Larger and highly connected to the cerebral cortex — especially the language centers of the cortex
Language centers	Few and poorly connected	Many and highly connected
Cingulate gyrus and emotional handling	Less connected to the cerebral cortex but better connected to the spinal cord	Highly connected to the cerebral cortex but less connected to the spinal cord
Hippocampus and emotive centers in the cerebrum	Small and less connected	Large and highly connected

Brain Chemistry for Dummies

Not only are the structures of his brain and her brain very different, but our brain chemicals are remarkably different too. Chemicals within the brain carry signals from one part of the brain (or from one neuron) to another — or from the body to the brain (and vice versa). More than *seventy* different chemicals have a major impact on the brain, affecting our emotions and responses. Two of the more interesting chemicals that affect the brain are hormones* and neurohormones,† which can impact his brain and her brain (and nervous system) in vastly different ways.

Testosterone

A male's major sex hormone, testosterone, impacts his behavior and moods. But as a mood regulator, testosterone is a midget when compared to a woman's major hormones — estrogen and

---

* A hormone is a chemical (usually a peptide or steroid) produced by one tissue and conveyed by the bloodstream to affect physiological activity (such as growth or metabolism) on another tissue.

† A neurohormone is a hormone secreted by or acting on a part of the nervous system.

progesterone. Nevertheless, testosterone is the hormone most associated with male aggressiveness, competitiveness, and assertiveness. A passive man, when given testosterone, will become more assertive and aggressive. Furthermore, competition raises testosterone levels, and rivalry fuels aggression. For example, testosterone levels among athletes are actually highest at the end of a competition rather than at the beginning.[8]

Testosterone, when given to a woman, will increase her aggression, but not as much as when given to a man, because his brain is hardwired to be more sensitive to this hormone. A woman's testosterone levels (and sexual appetite) increase at the time she ovulates. This surge lasts about forty hours. In contrast, a male's testosterone levels stay up at all times.

Testosterone also helps a man focus on a project, competition, mission, or venture. It keeps him from becoming distracted. Researchers at Georgia State University found that the "high performers" tested in each field (business leaders, politicians, sportsmen, and the like) had higher levels of testosterone.[9]

Testosterone makes the brain less liable to fatigue—more single-minded.[10]

Anne Moir, PhD

In addition, testosterone drives a man's desire for independence. Theresa Crenshaw, MD, an expert on sexual pharmacology, writes, "The 'loner profile' of testosterone is absolutely crucial to understanding what men are all about.... Testosterone motivates the male to strive for separateness in ways a woman is not.... It makes you want sex, but it also makes you want to be alone."[11]

When a wife says, "My husband is driven!" or "My husband is so independent!" or "My husband just won't give up or quit!" she is observing his testosterone at work. It stimulates the desire to succeed and achieve—to provide and protect. It stimulates his desire to conquer and to, at times, be alone. It also can lead to defensiveness and anger if she doesn't understand this and know how to approach him.

Oxytocin

This hormone is often called the "cuddle" or "bonding" hormone because it's released when couples hug and cuddle. This hormone increases sensitivity to touch and the feelings of bonding, especially in women. The higher the oxytocin levels a person has, the less aggressive and the more empathetic the person is. As you can guess, women tend to have much higher oxytocin levels than men.

Oxytocin stimulates in a woman's brain what biologists call the "tend and befriend" behaviors (as opposed to his brain's testosterone-driven "fight-or-flight" responses). When a woman feels highly connected to someone or something, this feeling, to a large extent, is enhanced by oxytocin. Oxytocin increases a woman's sexual receptivity and is partly responsible for her being able to have intense feelings of satisfaction during and after making love, even if she does not have an orgasm.[12] Oxytocin also increases a woman's warm and nurturing feelings toward her child and triggers her letdown reflex when breast-feeding. When a mother looks into the eyes of her baby, her oxytocin levels soar much higher than a man's, and this oxytocin rush is extremely pleasurable to a woman. In fact, the surge of oxytocin "feels better than good" to a woman, because "her core self, her core identity, is greatly fulfilled."[13]

There is, however, one time when the male's level of oxytocin approaches equality with a female's—during and immediately following orgasm during sexual intercourse. It's *his* moment of bonding and feeling that "oxytocin goodness." The phenomenon of oxytocin bonding increases the longer a man is with his wife. So for the male, monogamy actually can increase his bonding with and loyalty to his wife.

Vasopressin

Originating in the hypothalamus, this chemical, along with testosterone, regulates "sexual persistence, aggression, hierarchical displays and territorial markings."[14] Vasopressin can also foster parental behavior in males.[15] One reason men have higher levels of vasopressin than women is because the Y chromosome (found in males but not females) increases the density of vasopressin-producing fibers in males. During sexual foreplay, vasopressin is secreted in males but not in females (and men can be thankful for this because higher vasopressin levels in females actually lower a woman's sex drive).

> [*V*asopressin] is another reason that the care of infants is not and never will be dominated by men. Nor will first-grade classrooms ever be taught by more men than women. Those classrooms need higher levels of oxytocin, not vasopressin. High school classrooms are more likely to have more male teachers because adolescents are already more independent and thus may now need the kinds of aggression challenges that males bring to them.[16]
>
> **Michael Gurian**

Serotonin

Serotonin serves to calm us down. Men typically have far less serotonin than women, which is one reason they tend to act impulsively and react physically to a much greater degree than women. The combination of lower levels of serotonin and oxytocin and higher levels of testosterone and vasopressin biologically predisposes men to choose action first and talk second.

A woman's brain and moods are designed to be calmed by high levels of serotonin. Serotonin, when combined with high levels of oxytocin, lead women to become far more willing and capable than men to sit calmly and engage in conversation or child care.

The quieted impulsivity of serotonin … gives [females] the biological design advantage over men in finding bonding and nurturing behavior much more satisfying.[17]

Michael Gurian

Estrogen

When estrogen washes through her brain, a woman has an overall feeling of well-being and contentment. Estrogen has a calming effect and aids memory. Estrogen levels increase during the first half of the menstrual cycle, making a woman's brain more alert and sensitive to stimuli. It gives her brain feelings of higher self-esteem, enthusiasm, pleasure, and sexual arousal. As Dr. Anne Moir notes, it also makes women "superior in tasks requiring rapid, skillful, fine movements, as well as, of course, in everything requiring verbal fluency and articulation."[18]

A woman's hormonal changes during her monthly cycle, peri-menopause, or early menopause directly affect her brain function, especially during emotional experiences. These hormones affect not only her limbic system but also her brain hormones and functioning. Menopausal women, who have lower levels of estrogen yet still have some testosterone in their systems, naturally become more aggressive.

Progesterone

This hormone causes a woman to feel parental and nurturing, giving her an overall feeling of well-being and contentment. Like estrogen, it also has a calming effect and aids memory. Progesterone is a relaxant, so when levels plummet, as they do just before a woman's period (or after giving birth), a woman may feel more restless and have more difficulty with sleeping.[19]

In contrast, higher levels of progesterone can cause a woman's brain to become more sluggish, resulting in decreased libido and increased depression. This is typical during the second half of the menstrual cycle, when progesterone levels are higher.

Hormones control many aspects of a woman's physical and mental health. Women can have very different moods, needs, feelings, and symptoms at different times—and it's not just because they're trying to be difficult! Their hormones are literally changing how their female brain works. When their hormones go off-kilter, they can trigger anything from acne and insomnia to memory loss and weight gain. It's enough to ruin any couple's day—not to mention putting an increased strain on a marriage.

What Does It All Mean?

Table 3 summarizes the different chemical levels in his brain and her brain. These chemicals dramatically affect how his brain and her brain work.

Table 3 — Different Chemical Levels in His Brain and Her Brain

Chemicals	Male	Female
Oxytocin Serotonin Estrogen Progesterone	Low	High
Testosterone Vasopressin	High	Low

His brain's basic structure and function is established in the womb when the brain is bathed in testosterone. Then testosterone and vasopressin—all enhanced by his unique Y chromosome—step in to regulate a man's drives. This combination of brain structure and chemistry results in a brain prewired for competition and conquest.

For women, the connections in her brain, combined with elevated levels of oxytocin and another hormone associated with good feelings, dopamine—especially when having a conversation—result in feelings of great pleasure. This combination of brain structure and chemistry results in a brain prewired for conversation and connection with other people—hugging, cuddling, romance, and affection.

We hope this brief overview of the neuroanatomy and chemistry of his brain and her brain has given you some hints about the dramatic impact each can have on the stability, strength, and satisfaction of your marriage. The science clearly shows that there are two distinctly different brains.

- One is built for plans and pacts—the other for nurturing and networking.
- One emphasizes competition—the other compassion and caring.
- One is spatially and results oriented—the other conversation and cooperation centered.
- One gravitates toward projects—the other toward people.

Researchers have found many, many differences between his brain and her brain—and we predict they'll eventually find thousands more. The reason? His brain and her brain are complexly designed to be delightfully different and to respond in nearly opposite ways.

> *At* least 100 sex differences in male and female brains have been described so far. They keep cropping up in animal and human studies.[20]
>
> **Nancy G. Forger, PhD**

It's time to put to death the delusion* that his brain and her brain are the same. They are not and never have been. His brain and her brain are as different as night and day, and yet night and day tell us that our world is spinning properly—just as God designed it.

---

* A delusion is a fixed, false belief.

And that's a key point. It's no accident that God designed his brain and her brain to be *very* different. If we learn how to understand, appreciate, and honor these differences, we reap many benefits that will strengthen our relationship.

> *The* view that men are from Mars and women from Venus paints the differences between the two sexes as too extreme. The two sexes are different, but are not so different that we cannot understand each other.[21]
>
> **Simon Baron-Cohen, PhD**

Maybe that's why the apostle Peter instructs husbands to "live with your wives in an understanding way."[22] By discovering the many delightful differences between his brain and her brain, husbands and wives can grow in their appreciation and understanding of each other. This can lead to more realistic expectations of each other. Then frustration, disappointment, and anger can fade away as we discover that we can live together joyfully in marriage.

PART 2

The Differences

3

Chapter

Differences in How We Perceive Our World

BARB AND I ARE ALWAYS ENCHANTED BY THE GORGEOUS RAINBOWS we view from the front porch of our home. Usually illuminated against the dark clouds on the eastern horizon, the rainbow reminds us of God's everlasting love for us.[1] Every time we see one, we are amazed by God's glorious artistry.[2] It also reminds us of how differently men and women perceive the world.

> *W*omen can see colors and textures that men cannot see. They hear things men cannot hear, and they smell things men cannot smell.[3]
>
> **Leonard Sax, MD, PhD**

When I look at a rainbow, I see only seven colors (just like Isaac Newton did — red, orange, yellow, green, blue, indigo, and violet). However, Barb usually sees eight or nine colors in the rainbow. And when looking for paint colors for our bedroom, Barb considered a variety of greens — emerald, jade, verdant, olive, lime, and thirty-four other shades. I can look at the same colors and see only lighter and darker shades of green. I can see absolutely no difference between soft green and lily pad green — none! But for women, who have what researchers call "tetrachromacy,"* the difference in colors is glaring. Tetrachromat females can segment a rainbow into, on average, ten different colors.[4]

Differences in Sight

There are biological reasons for these differences. The retina receives light input and transfers it, via the optic nerve, to the brain. Rod-shaped cells (rods) on the retina are photoreceptors for black and white, while cone-shaped cells (cones) handle color. Women have a greater proportion of cones than men. So women can see colors better than men. No wonder many men tend to mismatch their shirts, ties, and socks!

Studies reveal that infant boys take in less sensory detail than infant girls. One study in England, looking at only two-to-four-day-old infants, found that girls spent almost twice as long as boys in maintaining eye contact with an adult, whether the adult was silent or talking.[5] Baby girls also observe and follow the eyes of an adult more often than baby boys[6] and make more eye contact than boys.[7]

But like every difference in the way males and females are designed, there are positives and negatives — strong spots and blind spots. Take night driving for example. A man's eyes are better designed for long-distance vision over a narrower field of vision — especially at night. Combined with his right-brained spatial ability, this allows a man to recognize and identify oncoming traffic much more quickly than a woman.

We men do see better than women in bright light, but we tend to see in a narrower field. In other words, we have what researchers call "mild tunnel vision — with greater concentration on

---

* Tetrachromacy is the condition of possessing four independent channels for conveying color information, or possessing four different cones, one other than normal RGB (red, green, blue).

depth."[8] This may be one reason that when it comes to child pedestrians who are killed or injured, boys outnumber girls by two to one. It's not just because boys are willing to take more risks (which they certainly do), but because they have poorer peripheral vision than girls.[9] A female's wider peripheral vision allows her to quite literally take in the bigger picture.[10] This eye design may also explain why female drivers are less likely to be hit from the side at an intersection when compared to male drivers.[11]

This design difference in the male/female eye also explains what happened one night when I was looking for an item in the bathroom. Barb had cleaned up the bathroom, and I was certain she had hidden an item from me. It was nowhere to be seen. I called to Barb, wanting to know where she had hidden it. Miffed at my blindness, she marched into the bathroom, and then, like magic, she grabbed the item from the top of the vanity—right where I had left it!

> *The* male brain takes in less sensory details than a woman's. That's why we don't notice dust, which apparently involves some kind of fine particles that settle on furniture. Men don't care about the inside of the house. We are wired for larger spaces, such as the garage, the driveway, the yard.[12]
>
> **Tom Purcell**

Early in our marriage, I was convinced Barb could do magic—producing the items I was searching for apparently out of thin air—whether in the refrigerator, my desk, or my workbench. Shazam! Presto!

Screwdrivers, dental floss, a stick of butter, car keys, wallets—through the years they've always been there. I just can't see them and Barb can. With her better peripheral and color vision, she can see the entire contents of the refrigerator without moving her head. With my tunnel vision, I have to move my head or eyes up and down and all around to locate a missing object.

The peripheral vision deficit that men have may also explain why they get caught turning to gaze at a beautiful woman. Men and women both look at attractive members of the opposite gender.[13] However, with men's relative tunnel vision, they have to turn their heads a bit, and even though the movement is almost imperceptible, they get caught nearly every time.

Male/female brain differences in perceiving are not limited to sight but occur in how we hear, feel, smell, and taste. We enjoy Rick David's tongue-in-cheek view of some of the biological differences in perception between males and females:

- The female brain, through the olfactory receptors, can smell one part per billion in detecting offensive odors. By the time the male notices anything reeks, it's too late.
- In women, the Hypo-Interferus Cortex is highly developed. This area of the female brain stimulates a desire to discuss family matters during the final minutes of tightly contested playoff games on TV.
- The "Frontal Sanitary Lobe" in males is missing.
- The "Thermomic Thalamus" tells the female that something is always wrong with the ambient room temperature and to change it by whatever means necessary.
- The "Pull-Over-I-Gotta-Go-Now! Gland" acts as a form of radar in women by releasing an uncontrollable unction to pee when being driven through gang-controlled portions of a city.[14]

If we expect our spouse to have our senses, we are in for a rude awakening.

Differences in Hearing

Researchers at McMaster University found that women possess a far greater density of nerves in an area of the brain associated with language processing and comprehension.[15] For example, one brain-imaging study showed that men listen with only one side of their brain but women use both.[16] Another brain study showed that women can listen to, comprehend, and process as many as seven separate auditory inputs (such as conversations) at the same time, whereas men can barely follow one.[17] One reason for this is a woman's larger corpus callosum, which connects her brain's left and right hemispheres and enables her to use several highly connected hearing centers in both sides of her brain simultaneously.

We women have an advantage over men when it comes to hearing. Simply put, women are better designed to receive and process multiple auditory inputs at the same time. When it comes to hearing, it appears that the hemispheres of a man's brain are connected by some very thin twine between two tin cans.

Hey, I resemble that remark! Anyway, I have to admit that Barb is better at both listening and hearing than I am. And in the vast majority of women, this is not a learned ability but an inborn skill. The innate differences in hearing ability can be demonstrated when boys and girls are very young. At one week of age, girls can distinguish their mother's voice from the sounds made by another baby. Boys can't.[18] Scientists who do this work have found that young girls can hear much softer sounds than those audible to young boys. Girls have a sense of hearing that is two to four times better than boys (depending on the frequency tested). This difference is present as early as children can be reliably tested.[19]

This helps explain why I could talk to a friend on the telephone at the same time I listened to the radio, to Kate reading out loud at the kitchen table, and to Scott and what he was watching on TV in another room! But when the phone rings at our home, Walt needs to turn off the TV, turn down the music, and ask the kids to be quiet before he can answer it. I just answer the phone.

In our house, a dripping faucet at night will wake Barb. However, even if I was awake and standing in front of the dripping faucet, I probably wouldn't notice. Women are not only better than men at hearing new sounds in their environment; they are also better at hearing higher-pitched sounds and are naturally more proficient in noticing small changes in volume and pitch.[20] This helps explain why mothers intuitively sing lullabies to girls but talk to (or play with) boys. It may also be part of the reason that six times as many girls as boys can sing in tune.[21]

The minor changes in tone and pitch also enable us to "hear" the emotions of children and adults. I can remember telling our son, Scott, "Don't use that tone of voice with me, young man." He was clueless as to how I could discern this.

Perhaps this is why Barb claims to be able to distinguish my tone of voice as well. Imagine—she thinks she can tell when I'm irritated on the inside and trying to be sweet to her on the outside!

With me, like the average male, one auditory input at a time is all my brain can handle. Knowing this helps me honor Barb by listening more carefully to her. For example, on a recent trip to the airport, Barb and I were listening to a CD. When Barb began to talk to me, I turned off the CD player. Barb said, "You don't have to turn that off." I smiled and said, "Oh yes I do, because I want to hear every word you say."

With all the inborn hearing advantages I have, plus the fact that my brain links sensory stimuli and memories, it's no wonder I remember a lot of what Walt has said from the moment we met. But Walt has trouble remembering half the items I asked him to pick up at the store yesterday!

Differences in Touch and Pain Sensation

His brain and her brain are not only different in hearing and vision, but from birth females react faster and more acutely to touch and pain. British researchers have found that women, when compared to men, feel more pain in more parts of the body more often and for a longer duration.[22] An adult woman's skin is at least ten times more sensitive to touch and pressure than a man's,[23] and contrary to popular belief, a woman's tolerance to pain is also lower.[24]

 *In* childhood and adulthood, tests that measure the skin sensitivity of males and females produce differences so striking that sometimes male and female scores do not even overlap. In fact, the most sensitive boys seem to feel less than the least sensitive girls.[25]

J. M. Reinisch, PhD

High oxytocin levels in women not only stimulate the desire to touch, but oxytocin also sensitizes the touch receptors of the skin. This fact explains why Western women are four to six times more likely to touch another woman during a conversation than a man is to touch another man.[26] And it also explains why a mother is not only more likely than a father to rush to the aid of a toddler who has fallen and is crying, but she is also more likely to touch, caress, or hug the child. No wonder we say things such as "staying in touch," "personal touch," "thin-skinned," or "so-and-so gets under my skin."

Bottom line: women are much more sensitive than men. Husbands would do well to remember that for a woman, a soft touch or a long, slow caress can go a long way.

Differences in Smell and Taste

When we say there are differences in smell and taste, we don't mean that a woman literally smells better but that her sense of smell (and taste, for that matter) is much better than a man's.

My tasting ability is much better than Walt's. And smell—let's not even go there. I used to think that his ignoring those stinky socks in the closet was just his way of trying to get back at me. Now I know that's not the case. He is just not built to smell or taste the way I can.

God designed each of us with at least ten thousand taste buds that discern sweet, salty, sour, and bitter, and we can taste these four qualities in all areas of the tongue.[27] Males are, even as newborns, better able to discern salty and sour tastes than women.[28] However, women have more taste buds and are significantly superior in tasting bitter and complex flavors.

When it comes to smelling (olfactory ability), women are truly in a different league from us guys—although this was only an anecdotal observation until recently.[29] Sensory researcher Pamela Dalton, PhD, and her team demonstrated that women of reproductive age were especially skilled at noticing low-threshold odors. With repeated exposure to a variety of smells, the women quickly got better and better at detecting odors. This increased sensitivity was five orders of magnitude greater for these women than for the men who were tested. The guys just couldn't detect the odors, even with practice. In other experiments, women did better than men at spotting a target odor against a background of other aromas, a setting more like real-world experience.[30]

Yale researchers have also demonstrated what every woman who has ever been pregnant knows—a woman's taste changes dramatically throughout her pregnancy.[31] A woman's sense of smell is also more acute during pregnancy. When I was pregnant with Kate and Scott, for example, I could smell odors that were in a building, such as the grocery store, even before I entered it. I also felt I could "smell" Walt's moods, and now researchers have shown that we ladies can smell our man's pheromones and unique musk—not just consciously but subconsciously too![32]

I've always wondered how Barb could enter our closet and tell that I had hung up a pair of pants I had worn many times without laundering—even before she found them!

If you think our physical senses are different, then just wait until you learn more about our thinking and processing abilities. How we process our experiences can be literally worlds apart.

4
Chapter

Differences in How We Process Input from Our World

BEFORE BARB AND I TOOK A WALK ONE AFTERNOON, I THREW ON AN OLD hat I hadn't worn in a while. When we returned home, we were having a glass of water when Barb sniffed and wrinkled her nose. "Let me see your hat," she requested. I handed her the hat, and she took in a deep breath. A big, contented smile crossed her face.

"What?" I asked.

"I smell last summer!" she exclaimed. "I smell the suntan lotion you used at the beach on our vacation. We had a great time, didn't we?"

I smiled too. We had had a great time. But I couldn't detect an odor coming from the hat. (And even if I had, I *know* I wouldn't have connected the odor with the memory in the same way Barb did.)

The differences in how our brains take in and process sensory information may lead us to believe that our spouse (or the entire other gender) is an alien being. Your spouse literally relates and responds to the world differently than you—and it's all due to the different ways his brain and her brain are designed to function. Understanding this is highly significant when it comes to a happy marriage.

Whenever Barb and I travel to another country, we research the history, culture, customs, and language of the people we will visit. By coming to understand a bit about their world—how they think and function—we're in a better position to enjoy the experience. In the same way, Barb and I want to introduce you to the way in which your spouse processes and relates to emotions, stress, and tasks at hand. Most likely it will be quite foreign to you.

Differences in Systemizing and Empathizing

Women are likely to spend hours happily engaged in conversations over coffee or tea, talking with neighbors or close friends, hosting potluck suppers, advising friends on relationship problems, shopping, or caring for friends, neighbors, or pets. When Barb and I are at an airport newsstand, she, like most women, is likely to flip through magazines featuring fashion, beauty, relationship advice, home decorating, gardening, and parenting.

I, like most of the men I observe, am more likely to look through magazines featuring computers, cars, boats, hunting, sports, electronics, and the outdoors. Men are more likely to spend hours happily engaged in projects (designing or figuring out how to improve something, whether in our workshops or at work, or in relation to our hobbies), independent activity (sports and outdoor ventures), or activities that encourage competition and dominance.

These behavioral and recreational preferences originate in the brain. Dr. Simon Baron-Cohen of Cambridge University has summarized these differences, "Males on average have a stronger drive to systemize, and females to empathize. Systemizing involves identifying the laws that govern how a system works.... Empathizing, on the other hand, involves recognizing what another person may be feeling or thinking, and responding to those feelings with an appropriate emotion of one's own."[1]

For example, girls as young as twelve months old respond more empathically to the distress of other people, showing greater concern through sadder looks, sympathetic vocalizations, and comforting.[2] Baron-Cohen points out, "The empathizer intuitively figures out how people are feeling, and how to treat people with care and sensitivity."[3]

On the other hand, the male brain functions best when it is analyzing, exploring, and constructing systems. Baron-Cohen tells us, "The systemizer intuitively figures out how things work, or what the underlying rules are controlling a system. Systems can be as varied as a pond, a vehicle, a computer, a math equation, or even an army unit. They all operate on inputs and deliver outputs, using rules."[4]

Not too long ago, we had a newlywed couple over for dinner. They expressed some challenges they were having with their relationship. The husband and I immediately launched into a discussion of the different causes and possible solutions to the problem.

I found myself empathizing with the young wife and the roller-coaster emotions she was experiencing. Walt's systemizing approach and my empathetic style were 100 percent different, yet both of us connected with the wife and husband in a meaningful way.

Systemizing Males, Empathizing Females

The systemizing and empathizing brain types manifest themselves in myriad ways:

- in the toys kids prefer (girls like human-like dolls; boys like mechanical trucks)
- in response to verbal impatience (females negotiate with others; males order others)
- in navigating (women personalize space by finding landmarks; men see a geometric system and take directional cues in the layout of routes)
- in play (girls cooperate; boys compete)[5]

Hara Estroff Marano

Differences in Spatial Skills

Another example of how his brain and her brain process differently is the way males and females handle spatial tasks — the ability to picture in 3-D the shape, dimensions, coordinates, position, location, proportions, movement, and geography of an object. Spatial processing involves being able to mentally rotate the object; reverse it; fly in, through, or around it; or turn it inside out. Navigating an obstacle course, reading a road map, and visualizing a topographical map or a blueprint in three dimensions are spatial skills.

Functional brain scans reveal that spatial ability for males is located in a specific and highly efficient area of the right hemisphere. In females, the highly connected hemispheres enhance verbal and emotional processing but hinder spatial processing. In fact, only about 10 percent of women have spatial abilities that are as good as the average male.[6]

> $\mathcal{J}$t is, for instance, true that most women cannot read a map as well as a man. But women can read a character better. And people are more important than maps. [The male mind, at this point, will immediately think of exceptions to this.].... The best argument for the acknowledgment of differences is that doing so would probably make us happier.[7]
>
> **Anne Moir, PhD**

This difference in spatial ability explains the difficulties that women have when reading maps. According to British mapmaker Alan Collinson, most women have difficulty navigating with maps "because they need a three-dimensional perspective to navigate a route." He explains, "I design tourist maps that have a three-dimensional perspective — they show trees, mountains, and other landmarks. Women have much greater success with this type of map." Why? "Our tests show that men have the ability to turn a two-dimensional map into a three-dimensional view in their mind, but most women don't seem to be able to do this."[8]

For a man, driving is a test of his spatial and math abilities, which allow him to drive in a way that appears dangerous to most women. When Walt is driving, it's been helpful for me to understand that what seems risky to me isn't as risky for him, given his brain design. Instead of nagging him by exclaiming, "Be careful!" or "Slow down!" I'll say, "Walt, I'd be more comfortable if you drove a bit slower." Then he can choose how to respond.

As I've come to realize how different my spatial skills are from Barb's — primarily by hearing her gasp when I change lanes in heavy traffic — I'm able to put her mind at ease by driving a bit slower. I make sure there is extra (although unnecessary) room between our car and the other (slowpoke) cars. The fewer gasps I hear, the better I'm doing!

Different Responses to Stress

His brain and her brain process and respond to stress in very different ways. His propensity to react with anger is now believed to originate from his brain connections that transport his emotional responses downward toward his body and physical responses. A woman's brain is more inclined to process her emotional responses upward to her brain's verbal, relational, and contemplation centers. So in response to stress, women tend to think and feel before acting. Men, on the other hand, seem to be hardwired to act first and deal with their thoughts later.[9] Feelings, if they come, are a distant third.

Part of the difference in crisis response is due to differences in the structure of connections within the brain; part is due to the impact of hormones. Drs. Ruben and Raquel Gur and their research team discovered that the portions of the brain used to control aggression and anger responses are larger in women than in men.[10] In addition, during crisis or stress, women do not get the enjoyable hormone surges of testosterone, vasopressin, and serotonin that men get by competing, fighting, or taking risks.[11] Rather, women are more likely to enjoy the surge of oxytocin they receive from involvement in conversation or caring relationships.[12]

Women will move toward tending and befriending—behaviors associated with higher levels of oxytocin and estrogen.[13] Tending involves creating a physically and emotionally safe and nurturing environment for our family and others. Befriending involves building relationships with others who can come alongside if we are unable to care for ourselves or our children.[14] We also receive comfort as we participate in activities with other women.[15] When my children were young, I always looked forward to picnic lunches at the playground with my girlfriends and their children. Activities such as these enhance the surges of oxytocin and other hormones we find so pleasurable.[16]

Professionals who reviewed early drafts of this book commented that we hadn't addressed the more competitive, results-oriented women we sometimes see in the professional world. Keep in mind that we are talking in generalities about his brain and her brain. As we said in the introduction, there are a large number of male-female differences, and any one difference will not apply 100 percent to you or your experience. However, for the majority of males and females, the research is fairly clear that from our earliest days in school and on into higher education, males tend to compete; females tend to cooperate.[17] There is no doubt that many women can be very competitive. However, their design is to cooperate, even when they compete.

For example, in law school, most women do not like the competitive nature of most of the classes.[18] Therefore, women tend to prefer courses that teach about mediation. And female lawyers are much more likely to seek positions with corporations or as judges.[19] Male lawyers are much more likely to choose positions as "criminal defense attorneys, the gladiators of the profession."[20] In stressful situations, "males don't just like competition more; they also do better when a situation is seen as competitive."[21]

Another study demonstrated a fact I saw when I attended medical school in the 1970s: if the atmosphere of a situation was perceived to be more competitive, the men did better, while the women did worse.[22] Other studies show the same: in competitive or stressful situations or times of crisis, in general, men not only enjoy competition more than women; they very often become more confident, while women may become more anxious.[23]

Women in Politics

The tendency for women to tend and befriend, and cooperate more often than compete, even in the highly competitive political world, could not have been better illustrated than in January 2007 when ABC's Diane Sawyer asked the sixteen women serving in the United States Senate how they would govern differently from the way men govern.[24] Here are four typical responses:

- "You will hear about collaboration, you will hear about cooperation, and you will hear about a format that I think brings people together."[25]
- "Women encourage ... more of an openness to process, to bring people together to the table ... collaboration and collegiality."[26]
- "[Women] tend to be much more inclusive."[27]
- "[Women] talk about how we are good at finding common ground."[28]

When under stress, men see aggression and risk taking as functional, while women see it as a problem.[29] When men respond physically to stress and realize what they consider to be positive results, such as when a man wins a competition, their testosterone and vasopressin levels and their feelings of satisfaction surge.[30]

For instance, when we were buying a home, the negotiation between the two real estate agents became tense and ugly. Immediately, I was ready for a fight. I was angry. After all, the seller's real estate agent had not been entirely truthful and had clearly violated a term of the contract. I began to plot for battle—knowing we had the upper hand.

I, on the other hand, had sensed the kind heart and sincere motivation of the woman who was selling the only home she had ever owned. I really felt for her and asked Walt if he would mind if I talked to her. Walt trusts my intuition, so he calmed down and agreed. When she and I talked, I discovered she was as upset as I was (mostly at the agents), so we agreed to meet. We talked over a cup of coffee—not just about the agents and the house but about our families and lives. By the end of our time together, the problem was resolved.

In another example, in a difficult real estate market we once received an extremely low offer for our home. I mean, in a buyer's market it's one thing to sell your house but another thing to give it away. But it *was* an offer. So I thought to myself, "Now let the negotiations begin!" I was ready to compete.

Do you see his brain at work? But my brain responded differently. I felt anxious and fretful. I was so ready to be done with it. I didn't want to negotiate or see our house remain on the market any longer. To me, selling for the offered price, even though it was very low, was a much less stressful option. Had I done that, we would have sold our home for far less than market value. But had Walt not controlled his impulse to compete—had he negotiated too aggressively—I think we would have lost the sale.

We talked about our different responses, and we agreed we would negotiate together. So we presented the potential buyer with a reasonable counteroffer during what turned out to be a pleasant visit that led to a substantially increased sales price.

Our responses to the exact same situations were totally different, yet together we were stronger as a team than we would have been apart. To me, these incidents were great examples of his brain and her brain working for a common goal but taking vastly differing routes! From our earliest days in life, in general, his brain leans toward competition, while her brain leans toward cooperation.

Different Emotional Responses

The amygdala, the "reacting" part of the brain located deep in the limbic system, handles emotional responses and aggressive impulses. It is connected to the frontal lobe in the "thinking" part of the brain, where impulse control and moral decision making are handled. Larry Cahill, PhD, a neurobiologist at the University of California, Irvine, and his colleagues found that amygdala works differently in men and women. This may provide another explanation for why women tend to be less aggressive than men.

The testosterone wash increases the size of the male's amygdala, and the larger the amygdala, the more aggressive the person tends to be. This is one of the reasons men, in general, tend to respond more physically, aggressively, or angrily to emotional stimuli than women. Also, a male's strong connections between his limbic system and his body make him more likely to act rather than talk. A woman's connection between the amygdala and the frontal lobe is much larger than a man's, so she is more likely to control her physical response to emotion.

The frontal lobe, which helps control emotions, is bigger in women than in men, so that women may be better able to filter out or suppress overly arousing feelings. According to Dr. Cahill, "That difference may be why women are less prone than men to fly off the handle."[31] Furthermore, since her connection between the amygdala and the emotive and language centers of the cerebral cortex is also much larger than a man's, she is also much more likely to want to talk about what she is feeling.

These facts explain why women recognize and process sensory input and emotions much more quickly than the average male. In fact, studies show that men can take up to seven hours longer, on average, than women to process emotional stimuli, thoughts, and feelings.[32]

Understanding this has been helpful for me. Knowing that men take much longer to process and deal with their feelings has given me the capacity to appreciate why Walt withdraws or becomes silent when he's upset or trying to decide something. Most of the time, I need to talk in order to process, but Walt needs time, space, and quiet. Then, to top it off, he not only has difficulty expressing his feelings in words, but he, like most men, takes much longer to process and express those feelings.

When men feel hurt or rejected, they may react physically by slamming a door or hitting or kicking something. Or they may react by withdrawing—going outside, to the workshop, or to the computer. At other times, he may react by "playing his cards close to the vest" and not revealing how he's feeling. He may not have had enough time to figure out what he is feeling. All of these biologically based behaviors can naturally lead to misunderstanding and conflict in a marriage. Why? When his wife is dealing with emotions, her nature is to talk about what's troubling her. When she does so, her brain produces more oxytocin—which has the effect of giving her a natural sort of high and helps relieve her stress and tension.

However, for a man, lengthy, emotionally charged talks can have the opposite effect. A woman who wants her husband to sit and talk may notice that he's showing signs of becoming irritable. He may be easily distracted, try to "fix the problem" quickly, or just walk away to do something else. If a female tries to talk to a male about their troubles before the man has had a chance to ruminate over them and process them, it can create as much stress for him as it would relieve stress for her. So when a husband and wife do talk, she would be wise to learn to respond to his overload signals. Michael Gurian has described some of these signals: "While talking, a man might become physically fidgety, or his eye contact might drift. He might interrupt, he might try to problem solve, or he might try to get out of the conversation so that he can go do something else, such as 'zoning out' in front of the TV or working on a project."[33]

Because men are uncomfortable talking about emotionally charged issues, they learn at a young age to mask or hide their feelings. It is important for women to understand these male brain realities because when a man masks his emotions, he usually does it as a biologic necessity. A husband's responses to emotion are not usually personal or directed at his wife. Rather, they are evidence of his unique design—providing a way to help him manage his emotions and the stress in his life and to protect his relationships.

When his brain and her brain process emotions, they do so in vastly different ways. Researchers have found that his brain processes emotion only on one side or the other of the brain, while her brain processes emotion in both hemispheres at the same time.[34] This fact means that a man can deal with logic or with words and use just his left brain. Or he can work to solve spatial problems while using just his right brain. But in either case, he can avoid activating any emotional center of the brain. However, in women, the areas of the brain that deal with emotions and emotional memories almost always operate at the same time as other brain functions. In other words, a "woman's emotions can switch on simultaneously with most other brain functions."[35]

So when men tell me, "My wife gets emotional about everything!" I say, "Bingo! Of course she does!" That's exactly how she's hardwired. She's designed to have this sensitivity—a sensitivity most men lack—to be our emotional eyes in a world in which we tend to be emotionally unaware. Not only that, her brain is *much* more skilled at mental juggling than his.

Differences in Multitasking

Drs. Ruben and Raquel Gur have used functional MRIs to show that women's brains light up in more areas and use more brain pathways than men's brains when given a variety of tasks.[36] Because a woman's brain is so highly interconnected when compared to a man's more compartmentalized brain, women are better designed to multitask. Not only is a woman's brain designed to multitask; it virtually never turns off.

Authors Shaunti and Jeff Feldhahn accurately describe a woman's multitasking ability:

> You're on your computer, moving between six or seven open screens on your desktop. Perhaps you're juggling three or four Word documents, an Excel spreadsheet or two, and your home budgeting program. It's a digital Grand Central Station. Now add another dimension: Imagine that some of the open files and programs are actually weeks old and have been running in the background the whole time. Even worse, your computer is infected with spyware that keeps causing annoying advertisements to pop up. You've tried to close these unwanted files and pop-ups many times. You've installed anti-spyware programs and rebooted your computer. But those pesky things just keep coming back.[37]

Jeff then concludes, "Welcome to a woman's mental and emotional world."

You only have to go to your local restaurant to see this happening. When families with young children eat out, the wife will feed the infant in the high chair, watch the toddler in a booster seat, talk to her husband about his day, and ask the waiter to bring more napkins—all while feeding herself. The husband just concentrates on the task at hand—eating his meal.

The brains of women seem to be well "networked," while the brains of men are much more "compartmentalized." This phenomenon is vividly captured in the word picture evoked by the title of Bill and Pam Farrel's book *Men Are Like Waffles — Women Are Like Spaghetti*.[38] Men tend to process in "one waffle box" at a time, while a woman's processing tends to be highly convoluted and interconnected — like "spaghetti."

Barb and I have seen the value of our single-focus and multitasking abilities working together during a family emergency. One year we were preparing Easter Sunday dinner when we heard a crash, then a scream and a cry for help.

We knew instantly that our thirteen-year-old son, Scott, was in trouble — big trouble. Barb and I ran to the garage. Scott had been trying to carry his bike up some stairs when he fell. He was curled up on his side, crying. Blood was pouring out of his leg.

My medical training kicked in. I rushed to Scott's side and quickly examined the wound. The chain drive sprockets of his bike had sliced through the skin of the back of his knee all the way down to the large popliteal artery.

I put pressure on the wound with my hand and called to Barb, "Get a towel! We need to get to the ER." I turned to reassure my son he was going to be OK.

After grabbing a clean towel for Walt, I told Kate to get in the car, called a friend to activate our church's prayer chain, turned off the oven, sprinkled cleanser on the blood on the floor, and locked the front door. After Walt carried Scott to the car, we drove to the ER. As Walt took care of Scott in an exam room, I kept Kate occupied, filled out forms, called my mom, and then planned how I would finish cooking dinner.

Meanwhile, I was caring for Scott. Thankfully, the large artery had not been compromised, and I sewed up his laceration in the ER.

Walt's brain responded calmly in the crisis, and his ability to focus allowed him to take care of the problem at hand. My multitasking brain directed me to do things he never would have considered. My brain and his brain working together did a better job than either of us would have done alone.

Differences in Intuition

When a friend told me he admired my good judgment, I remembered the old saying that good judgment comes from experience and experience often comes from bad judgment. One of my worst bad judgments came from not valuing my wife's advice and intuition when making a large investment early in my professional career.

After beginning in private practice, Barb and I decided it was time to apply some of the financial principles we had learned from the Bible. We had always been good stewards in the sense of tithing, giving, and budgeting, but now was the time to begin to invest for the retirement years.

During this time Walt was presented with what he thought was a wonderful retirement plan. For reasons I still cannot explain, I did not think it was so wonderful.

"Why not?" he asked me.

I said, "I don't know. It just doesn't feel right to me."

So Walt spent quite a bit of time with charts, graphs, and data trying to convince my left brain why this was the correct investment for us. I patiently listened. I understood what he was saying, I really did—but all I could sense were red flags. Maybe because I admire Walt's intellect and understand his risk-taking nature, I didn't insist he see it my way. However, I told him in no uncertain terms that I didn't think it was a good idea.

My rational left brain, unable to effectively communicate with my right brain, decided not to listen to Barb or to be sensitive to the intuitive response that came from the complex connections between her right and left brains. So I made the investment.

And guess what? It went belly-up in world-record time. By not listening to and honoring Barb's unique processing power, I almost drove us into bankruptcy. We spent the next five years digging out of that debt.

I learned the hard way not to second-guess the subconscious processing power of my wife. I learned to take her intuition seriously—to value and honor it—and, as a result, I live with far fewer conversations ending with, "I told you so!"

My point is this: Barb perceived something I did not and responded exactly as she was designed—as only *she* could. If I had valued Barb's unique design—if I had understood that her intuition was designed to dovetail with a blind spot that I had, even though I never would be able to understand it, I would have avoided a disaster.

This story shows how very differently men and women interpret, make judgments about, and relate to the world around us. A woman's brain is designed to recognize subtle details in a person's eyes, body movement, facial expression, and tone of voice. Her ability to subconsciously process a multitude of observations allows her to judge a person's character and attitudes more rapidly and accurately than he can—and it can be documented very early in life.

> *Intuition is truly a feminine quality, but women should not mistake rash conclusions for this gift.*[39]
>
> **Minna Antrim**

Even before girls can understand language, they seem to be better than boys at identifying the emotional content of speech and facial expressions.[40] They are more sensitive to reading facial expressions and better at decoding nonverbal communication. Baby girls, for example, prefer to gurgle at people, but boys are just as content to gurgle at toys or mobiles.[41] And when viewing equal numbers of images of people and objects, girls will remember seeing people; boys will remember seeing objects.[42] No wonder some researchers now believe that what we've called a woman's intuition may just be her natural ability to notice small details and changes in the appearance or behavior of others. One author observes, "It is obvious to a woman when another woman is upset or feeling hurt, while a man generally has to physically witness tears or a temper tantrum or be slapped on the face before he even has a clue that anything is going on."[43]

So it's no wonder that when Walt and I walk into a gathering, I am almost instantly able to read the relationship between each couple in the room. I can tell who has had, or is having, an argument, who is competing with whom, who is happy with whom, who is making an advance on whom. Walt's still trying to remember the name of the couple sitting on the couch over there. I not only remember their names; I also know how most of them are feeling.

That's one reason most men simply can't lie to most women. If they try, she can pick it up in a nanosecond. For example, early in our marriage, we were visiting various churches in order to find a church home. One Sunday, when Barb was out of town, I visited one that I thought was right up our alley.

The next Sunday, we visited the church together. Walt loved the pastor, the people, the teaching, and the fellowship. But my immediate impression was overwhelming—that the pastor was slick, trying too hard to impress, and trying to put one over on us. I didn't trust him any farther than I could throw him.

A few years later, we learned that this man had been accused of frequently plagiarizing sermons and of padding his curriculum vitae with education and certifications he never obtained.

I was never able to explain to Walt the origin of my mistrust and suspicion, but it was an impression I never doubted. The Bible teaches that God will "give you a wise and discerning heart" and "very great insight."[44]

And more often than not, this wisdom and great insight come to a husband from his wife. Wise is a man who understands, appreciates, and honors this unique quality his wife has been given.

When it comes to how we process, his brain and her brain *are* different. Table 4 summarizes some of our unique differences.

Table 4 — Different Brain Types and Processing

Brain Type and Processing	His Brain	Her Brain
Brain type	Highly systemized	Highly empathetic
Ability to compartmentalize	High	Low
Ability to multitask	Low	High
Ability to control emotions	High	Low
Relational oriented	Low	High
Project oriented	High	Low
Ability to "zone out"	High	Low
Response to stress	Fight or flight; act first and think later	Tend or befriend; think and feel before acting
Response to risk	Aggressive	Cautious
Response to same sex	Compete	Cooperate

Remember that we're talking about generalities here. We realize there may be exceptions to the information contained in table 4, even in *your* marriage. Take note of the exceptions, but notice that most of these differences are likely to apply to most men and women—and that is good.

> *A* woman uses her intelligence to find reasons to support her intuition.[45]
>
> **Gilbert K. Chesterton**

Louann Brizendine, MD, observes, "Being a woman is like having giant, invisible antennae that reach out into the world, constantly aware of the emotions and needs of those around you."[46] Understanding this allows me to comprehend and appreciate how Barb reaches her conclusions. I now know that her larger corpus callosum and increased volume of white matter combine to give her a vast complex of conscious and unconscious connections between her right and left brain. This remarkable design gives her antennae into our world that I simply do not have—an internal radar system, if you would, that I now value and for which I am deeply grateful.

5

Chapter

Differences in How We Communicate
with Our World

PASTOR DAVE STRODER PENNED A HUMOROUS STORY ABOUT HOW MEN
and women communicate in different ways:[1]

My wife, Kristie, and I were on our way to a Sunday school
picnic, and looked forward to a day of fun with people from
our church. Sunny skies, delicious barbecue, cheerful conversation, and, of course, potato chips. That was our job, to bring
those blasted chips.

As we drove to the party in my wife's sporty convertible,
we pulled into a small Food Mart to fulfill our assignment.
She said something about what to purchase, and I nodded.

I don't remember what she said. That's because I didn't
listen. I'm a grown man; I think I can handle picking out potato chips.

I returned to the car, threw the bag in the back, and hopped
in, ready to enjoy the lovely day, when my wife asked, "What
kind of chips did you get?"

"Huh?"

"Did you buy the chips I asked you to get?"

"You told me to get a certain kind?"

"You never listen to me!" she said.

"Who *cares* what kind of chips I got? They're *chips*! I think I'm capable of buying potato chips," I said, sure this defense would win the argument.

It didn't.

She pressed the issue.

And that's when I made an executive decision: "Let me out right here!"

"No problem!" She slammed on the brakes.

Even before we completely stopped, I jumped free of the fight, the car, and the potato chips. Then I watched Kristie speed toward home.

Boy, I showed her! I thought. And then I looked around.

Piece of advice: Before you demand to get out of a car, check to see exactly where you are. As I scanned the area, I realized I was standing on a lonely wooded road miles from anywhere. The picnic was in a forest, and there was no civilization within a ten-mile radius.

Several hours and five miles later, sweaty, blistered, and with feet and legs I was sure would never work again, I arrived home. Although the house was quiet, I knew where to find my wife—asleep in bed. That was her usual way to process conflict.

I stood and looked at her. I wasn't angry anymore; I was barely conscious.

She woke enough to return the gaze. I could tell she wasn't angry either. Then humbly I said those two important words, "Move over."

Exhausted, I climbed into bed next to her, too tired to speak, but desperately wanting to reconnect. We laid there silently until we both escaped into a much needed sleep.

When we awoke, Kristie said, "I see you made it home all right." Those words held a glimmer of compassion.

"It took a while." Pause. "But I needed to cool off," I finally admitted.

"Did anyone see you?" A smile crept across her face.

"No. I managed to dive into some bushes just before the Wallaces' Toyota turned the corner. I got cut." I pulled back the blanket to reveal a swollen cut and bruised area on my leg.

"Oh, Honey!" she exclaimed and jumped into action. Running to the bathroom sink, she grabbed a washcloth and hurried back to the bed. I smiled at how quickly I'd won her over — until I noticed she was cleaning the sheets rather than caring for my leg.

Well, at least we're talking, I thought, a little hurt.

Then I knew I had to take the first step, to be quick to reconcile. *I hate this part,* I half thought, half prayed.

"Listen," I started. "I'm sorry about earlier."

"What exactly are you sorry about?" she asked. I could see she wasn't going to let me get away with an undefined apology. "What exactly are you asking me to forgive?"

OK. I should know this. How hard could it be?

"I'm sorry for buying the wrong potato chips," I said with my best puppy-dog eyes.

Her stare hardened. One eyebrow raised. I'd obviously missed the mark.

"No, David, the potato chips are not the problem."

"Then what is?"

Fortunately Kristie knew that the line "I shouldn't have to tell you" doesn't work on clueless guys like me. I need a picture drawn carefully if I'm going to get the point.

"You didn't listen," she began. "When you disregard what I suggest ... I feel as if my opinion isn't important to you. I feel as if I don't matter. It's not about the potato chips; it's about how you value me. Yes, the chips are a minor irritation, but I asked specifically for something and you blatantly ignored it."

I sat for a moment to let her words sink in, then as carefully as possible I repeated what I'd heard. "So you really aren't against barbecue-flavored chips?" She nodded, then waited for more.

I took a deep breath. "So if I'd simply asked you to repeat what you'd said, I would have known what you wanted, and more important, I would have shown you respect because I took the time to listen to you and your opinion?" I waited for the verdict.

Did I get it right this time? I wondered.

Kristie didn't say a word. She applauded. A new smile crept across her face. Now that she'd been heard, she rewound the mental tape of what happened and owned up to her part. "I'm sorry too."

"Really? For what?" I wasn't about to make it simple for her.

"I overreacted. It was just a bag of chips, and I turned it into a drama. I could have talked to you about it later and supported your barbecue choice. I probably made you feel disrespected by treating you like a child. Now we missed the picnic and you got injured on the walk home." Finally she used the washcloth on my leg.

"Will you forgive me?" It was her turn with the puppy-dog eyes.

"Will you forgive me?" I asked her.

"Of course," we said in unison.

———

When we realize how differently our brains work, it's no wonder that communication between husbands and wives can be a challenge. "The failure of communication [between the genders] is one of the basic facts of life," writes Dr. Anne Moir. "In the light of our new understanding [of male and female brains], it seems absolutely predictable that women should fret at men's lack of communication—because men's brains are not structured that way."[2] Her brain is simply designed to process and enjoy verbal communication more than his brain.

What Did You Say?
Our Biology Makes a Difference

We come into the world with differences in how we hear and speak already in place. The effect of testosterone in the unborn male changes his brain so that it has fewer and less connected verbal centers than does her brain. So it should not surprise us that girls develop proficient language skills earlier than boys do.

We can see evidence of these differences by the time children are toddlers. Not only do girls say their first words earlier than boys; they also tend to speak in longer sentences earlier. These differences are so profound that by three years of age the average girl has twice the vocabulary of the average boy—and her speech, compared to his, is nearly 100 percent understandable.[3]

What is happening in the brain to cause these differences? Women use specific areas located on both sides of the brain for speech and language functions, while men tend to use just one side of their brain (the left hemisphere) for verbal tasks. This fact has been documented in a study in which volunteers listened to a passage from a John Grisham novel. The team used functional MRIs to map areas of the brain that were the most active during passive listening. They found that females used both hemispheres of the cortex, while the males used only the left hemisphere.[4] Findings in other functional imaging studies have shown that when men read, just a small area in the left hemisphere (the left inferior frontal gyrus) lit up. In women, both frontal lobes lit up, and the activation was much more diffuse.[5]

Research on the impact of strokes helps confirm the significance of these differences in language processing. When women have stroke damage to one hemisphere or the other, their scores on vocabulary and verbal fluency tests are only slightly affected. In men, however, vocabulary and verbal fluency scores are only affected when there is damage to his left hemisphere.[6]

So who really does talk the most—men or women? Barbara and Allan Pease state, without citing any sources, that "a woman can effortlessly speak an average of 6,000–8,000 words a day. She uses an additional 2,000–3,000 vocal sounds to communicate, as well as 8,000–10,000 facial expressions, head movements, and other body language signals. This gives her a daily average of more than 20,000 communications.... [A man] utters just 2,000–4,000 words and 1,000–2,000 vocal sounds, and makes a mere 2,000–3,000 body language signals. His daily average adds up to around 7,000 communication 'words'—just over a third the output of a woman."[7]

We have located many similar claims, with estimates of women using anywhere from 7,000 to 50,000 words a day and men using anywhere from 2,000 to 25,000 words a day. There are two things these authors have in common: (1) they claim women use two to three times as many words in a day as a man, and (2) we can find no actual research to support their claims.

However, assertions that women talk more than men may be an urban legend. One writer who has researched this legend concludes, "Nowhere could I find any evidence that anyone has ever supported these assertions by actually counting words or measuring talking times."[8]

One group that reviewed this topic reported, "It is shown that the widely held belief that women talk more than men is unsupported in the literature. Of the studies reviewed that examined mixed-sex interaction, the majority found either that men talked more than women, or that there was no difference between men and women in amount of talk."[9]

The most recent study, published as we were completing this book, was based on researchers who used digital voice recorders over an eight-year period to count how many words 396 college students spoke during an average day. The students carried the voice-activated digital recorders that sampled their speech for several days. Their daily word use was calculated from the number of recorded words. The study found that men and women both spoke an average of about 16,000 words a day.[10]

However, as we might have expected, the researchers did find some communication differences between the genders, which centered primarily on the subjects men and women discussed. Men talked more about technology and sports, while women talked more about their relationships. The researchers found that women relied more on pronouns such as *I*, *she*, and *we*, while men tended to use articles such as *a* and *the*. "It really reflects what they're interested in," said one of the researchers. "You only use articles when you're talking about concrete things. Women talk about people. Men talk about tools and carburetors."[11]

The Emotional Link

When it comes to talking, women are naturally good at it, enjoy it, and do a lot of it. In addition, the neural connections between a woman's emotional processing and memory centers are larger, far more active, and more strongly connected to the verbal center of the brain than in a man. She is designed to connect memories, words, and feelings, and so her conversation tends to be laden with emotion and meaning.

Not so with men. The biologic design of men causes them to be less likely to identify and communicate their emotions. With a smaller hippocampus, men remember fewer emotional experiences than women. Furthermore, the portions of his brain that process emotion are much smaller and much less connected than those in her brain. So a man's capacity to feel and express emotions is physically separated from his ability to verbally express them. In conversation, men are much less likely (or even able) to talk about emotions and generally express much less emotional content than the average woman. This fact explains why male conversations are usually filled with facts and are devoid of emotion.

> *The* reluctance men have with feeling and with communicating emotions has a biological root. Their capacity to feel is, to a greater degree than in women, physically divorced from their capacity to articulate; further, the emotional centers of the male brain are located far more discretely than in the woman.[12]
>
> **Anne Moir, PhD**

When Barb is upset or concerned about an issue, she wants to talk with someone and vent. When I'm upset, I don't need to vent verbally. I need to think, not talk. When facing emotional situations or problems to be solved, Barb's brain is designed to talk to others, while my brain is designed to talk to itself.

Functional brain scans show that when a man wants to talk to someone, his left hemisphere becomes active, as though it is searching for a verbal center but can't find one. Consequently, husbands are not as verbally able as their wives. In addition, the cortical processing areas that men use for solving puzzles or problems tend to be the same regions that women use for emotive processing.[13]

So when he's dealing with a project, a problem, a stress, or an emotion, a man will typically become very quiet. While using his right brain to solve problems or deal with emotions, it is hard for a man to use his left brain to listen or speak. His compartmentalized brain is designed to do one thing at a time; it is difficult for him to solve a problem and converse at the same time. Scans show that when a man is sitting silently, his brain is either at rest or he's "having a conversation with himself."[14]

Most women find it incomprehensible—and even frightening—if they don't realize that this is how a male's brain is designed to work. It's almost the opposite of her brain. A woman's brain is *never* at rest, and when she is dealing with a problem, she not only *wants* to talk but also *needs* to talk. Her conversation with another person allows her to reduce stress and talk through the problem. It's important for men to realize that when she does this, she's not necessarily looking for a solution in the same way he would.

A good example occurred while we were writing this book. During a late spring snowstorm, we took a coffee break and spent a few moments gazing at the large, fluffy flakes of snow that were falling. A number of things were racing through my mind: Would we finish the book on time? Who was I going to hire to do some sheetrock work at our new home? Who would I get to help us move? Was the color I had chosen for the dining room too dark? I was sure *Walt also had a lot going on in his mind. "What are you thinking?" I asked him.*

"Nothing," he replied.

I was surprised, because there was so much going on in our lives. I thought surely he would be thinking about something. I know I always have *something on my mind—or actually, several things on my mind. But he just sat there, thinking nothing and enjoying the snow.*

The fact is that his brain and her brain perceive the world quite differently and communicate in very different ways. We speak and hear language differently. We mean different things by what we say. As a result, a significant communication gap can build up between us and divide us if we're not aware of our design differences and why they are there. To bridge this communication gap, we need to understand not only how we say what we say but also what the other gender's brain hears.

Coming to recognize and understand our communication and language differences has allowed Barb and me to smile and laugh more as we work to build a stronger marriage. In our next chapter, we'll share some of what we've learned about successfully bridging this chasm.

6

Chapter

Decoding Our Communication Differences

IT'S PERFECTLY NATURAL FOR A WOMAN TO WANT TO TALK ABOUT HER FEELINGS and emotions with the man in her life. It's also perfectly natural for this man to avoid extended conversation as much as possible—particularly if it is emotionally focused. Given these opposite starting points, it should come as no surprise that the most common dissatisfaction in marriage for a woman, at least after a few years, is that her husband doesn't provide the conversation she needs.[1]

The statistics on this problematic communication gap are staggering:

- Ninety-eight percent of women want their man to talk to them more about their own "personal thoughts, feelings, plans, emotions, and questions."[2]
- Seventy-four percent of working women say their biggest disappointment with their husbands is their "reluctance to talk, particularly at the end of the day."[3]
- Eighty-one percent of women said they have to initiate most of their conversations and that they have a very hard time getting men to express their innermost thoughts.[4]

As you may have guessed, a woman's sensitivity to this communication gap has a biological origin—the calming, feel-good, bonding hormone called oxytocin. This hormone compels a woman to find others with whom she can "talk it out," because when she does, it feels good and helps relieve stress and tension. Conversation with her husband is especially important because it magnifies the feelings of bonding and intimacy that she longs for in her relationship with him.

> *J*ust as [a husband] finds sex enjoyable in its own right, [a wife] needs conversation. As with most women, it makes her feel more romantic love for [him] because she can deeply share her life with her husband. The atmosphere it creates contributes much to her happiness. The man who takes time to talk to a woman will have an inside track to her heart.[5]
>
> **Willard F. Harley, PhD**

However, if a wife's expectation is that her husband will be the sole provider of oxytocin-rich relationships and conversations, she is likely to feel unloved and quite alone. She may expect her husband to be available and able to meet all of her emotional and conversational needs, but it's just not the way he is built!

His brain is built to see conversation as a means to an end, whereas her brain is designed to see talking as an end in itself. Women bond through conversation and give support by listening. They define themselves, at least in part, by the quality of their relationships and conversations. So for a woman, talking is not optional, even though her husband is not designed with the same need or capacity to listen.

Researchers have found that not only is her brain built to listen more acutely than his brain, but a woman can use up to six "listening expressions" on her face in any ten-second period of conversation.[6] Whether women are speaking or listening, they reflect in their faces what they are feeling. A woman's facial expressions communicate feelings to such an extent that when two women are talking to each other, it can be very difficult to tell who is sharing and who is responding.

Guys, on the other hand, tend to listen with almost no facial expressions. However, the man who learns both to listen to *and* reflect his wife's feelings in his facial expressions will create very, very strong bonds with his wife. Men may be "daunted by the prospect of using facial expressions while listening, but it pays big dividends for the man who becomes adept at the art."[7]

Barb and I have come to understand these differences and have learned to love each other well by understanding how we each communicate. When Barb and I were writing this book, for example, we were also looking for a new home. Barb took the lead in looking at candidate homes, and during the process she'd sometimes feel stress or pressure. When she did, she needed time just to talk.

For me, talking about all of the available houses I was looking at was very rewarding, and Walt was wise enough to just listen to me. I didn't want or need him to click into his normal problem-solving mode. I just needed to talk and cuddle until I felt relaxed and comfortable again.

I feel blessed that Walt will do this, because many husbands view listening to their wife talk as an official waste of time. After all, men are built to fix things, complete the project, and move on. Walt is built that way too. When he's stressed, he'll do something — organize his tools, take a walk, play solitaire on his computer, or watch a game on TV. But he also has learned that when I'm stressed, I want and need to talk.

Husbands and wives would be wise to understand and pay attention to these communication opposites. It can be highly rewarding to develop strategies for better communication. It makes no sense for women to assume or expect men to communicate in the same way they do.

Raging at men's innate maleness is as useful as raging against the weather, or the existence of the Himalayas; we believe it is rather more sensible to put on a raincoat, and abandon plans to bulldoze Everest.[8]

Anne Moir, PhD

Men Speak the Language of Action

It has been helpful for Barb and me to learn that a man is designed to transform "emotion into an idea that can be managed safely."[9] A man's high levels of testosterone and vasopressin lead him toward problem-solving responses to stressors. So a man's brain and hormones compel him to respond to emotions and stress by either doing something or fixing something. They lead him toward aggression and action, dominance and decision making.

Dr. Anne Moir describes perfectly how this affects the way a man naturally seeks to communicate with his wife: "The language of the male is more in the vocabulary of action—doing things, sharing activities, expressing feelings through inarticulate gifts, favors, and physical courtesies. Holding a door open or carrying in the groceries is not a mere social convention; it is the masculine for 'I care for you.' "[10]

When a couple does not understand this dynamic, it can lead to great miscommunication, as it did for newlywed friends of ours.

The wife complained to her husband that he did not show a loving attitude toward her. His response was to plant flowers and trim the lawn for her. She still was not happy, so he painted the family room for her.

That didn't help, so he bought tickets to a Denver Broncos' game. He couldn't imagine a date that would be more fun for the two of them than to go to a professional football game. When he told her about the tickets, she broke down crying. He was flabbergasted and reacted defensively. Before long, they showed up at our home in the middle of a major argument.

As we talked, it became clear that his yard work and painting were all attempts to show her how much he loved her. The Bronco tickets were the capstone—the best thing he could think of to do with his best friend, his wife. She had no idea that his actions were expressions of love and care; she was simply frustrated that he didn't seem to know that what she wanted most was for him to sit down and listen to her.

 To prove his love for her, he climbed the highest mountain, swam the deepest ocean, and crossed the widest desert. But she left him—he was never home.[11]

Barbara and Allan Pease

Earlier in our marriage, Barb and I struggled in similar ways. When Barb talked about challenges she was experiencing, I thought she was giving me a list of problems she expected me to fix. The longer she talked, the more uncomfortable I would become. Listening to her talk for long periods of time was not only unnatural but painful. Why? Men simply are not built to listen to people talk ad infinitum about problems—we're built to do something about them.

Women Thrive on the Language of Relationship

Although I love that Walt has learned how important it is to listen and talk with me, I also understand that my Creator's design for him and for me is for me to find other women with whom I can build emotional bonds and relationships. I enjoy and need prolonged conversation in my life—something that Walt is not built to provide.

I was relieved to understand that I was *not* equipped or designed to meet or satisfy all of Barb's emotional needs. She *and* I need her to have meaningful and satisfying relationships with and spend time with other women. In fact, researchers have found that couples have better marriages when wives make up for conversation deficits with their husbands through their female friendships.[12]

That is why it is important for me to make time to relate to other women. Female friends and fellowship are essential to my emotional health.

> *It* seems to us quite natural that the closest friend of most women should be another woman, because women's biology places a premium on relationships, and like attracts like.[13]
>
> **Anne Moir, PhD**

Barb and I are, and for thirty-seven years have been, each other's best friend. However, for some reason, I've always understood that Barb needed female friends with whom she could interact and talk. I've seen that it's been healthy not only for her but also for our relationship and marriage. I find that some men I counsel don't understand this basic his brain/her brain principle, namely, that a woman needs to be able to talk to other women to be emotionally healthy. Even so, this truth hasn't let me off the hook in terms of wanting and needing to learn how to talk to and listen to Barb when she needs me.

I have encouraged Walt to spend more time talking with me and have been encouraged as he has learned to express his deepest feelings to me. Nevertheless, it's been much more fruitful for me to accept our unique designs and seek to fulfill many of my conversation needs with other women. A woman who tries to change her husband's design usually ends up feeling more and more alone because he is not equipped to completely satisfy her emotional need for prolonged conversations.

*N*othing less than her safety and the health of her relationship and family may depend on her developing oxytocin-based relationships with other women ... with whom she can more fully develop her own emotional world and thus depressurize her emotional relationship with her partner.[14]

Michael Gurian

Deciphering Indirect Talk

Women do not use language as literally as men. For them, precise definitions are irrelevant—it's what they feel that's more important. So poetic license and exaggeration are not uncommon in a woman's speech repertoire. Women are, in fact, experts at indirect talk—conversation that overflows with emotion and meaning.

Indirect talk is virtually never a problem when used with other women. The type of language that women use often will include qualifiers such as "sort of," "some," "kind of," "could you?" "a bit," "always," and "every"—along with many others. Women instinctively pick up the real meaning of another woman when she uses this type of talk. These words build rapport and relationship among women. But it can be disastrous with men.

Men are much more direct, concrete, and factual in verbal communication. Because men tend to have and use only one verbal center, which is poorly connected to their emotional processing center, men tend to use fewer words and shorter sentences to communicate. Men take and mean words literally. "Say what you mean and mean what you say" is a mantra by which most men communicate. Such language is almost never a problem when men talk to men. Our speech tends to use qualifiers like "none," "absolutely," "never," "will you?" and "when will you?" among others. But such language can be problematic when a man talks to a woman.

What Women Say and What They Mean

Men, who pride themselves on saying what they mean, are often confused and mystified by the indirect language women often use. To help men out, a humorous commentary on the difference between what women say and what they mean makes these observations:

- When a woman says, "That's OK," this is one of the most dangerous statements she can make to a man. "That's OK" means that she wants to think long and hard before paying you back for whatever it is that you have done. At some point in the near future, you are going to be in some mighty big trouble.[15]
- When a woman says, "Fine," this is the word she is using to end an argument when she feels she is right and you need to shut up. Never use "fine" to describe how a woman looks.
- When a woman says, "Five minutes," this means "half an hour." It is equivalent to the five minutes that your football game is going to last before you take out the trash, so it's an even trade.
- When a woman says, "Nothing," this means "something," and you should be on your toes. "Nothing" is usually used to describe the feeling a woman has of wanting to turn you inside out, upside down, and backwards. "Nothing" usually signifies an argument that will last "five minutes" and will end with the word "fine."

How does the direct versus indirect communication battle play out in our lives? Here is an example that takes place in our marriage on a weekly basis. Our garbage is collected on Tuesday mornings. There is a set of statements I could use every Monday evening. This list moves from indirect (more likely to be used by and understood by me) to direct (more likely to be used by and understood by Walt). Perhaps you will hear echoes of conversations that take place in your home:

- *Do you feel like taking the garbage out tonight?*
- *Wouldn't it be good if the garbage was taken out this evening?*
- *Do you think the garbage should be taken out?*
- *Would you please take the garbage out?*
- *Will you take the garbage out?*
- *Take the garbage out now!*

Walt could literally answer "yes" to each of the three first statements and still not move or take the garbage out — even though he's usually happy to do this for me.

So when Barb asks me, "Can you take the garbage out?" I tend to take her words literally. Of course, I *can* take the garbage out. I'm strong enough. I know how to. So to answer her question with a yes does *not* actually meet her need or answer her question.

I can choose to get mad or irritated, I can choose to nag, or I can choose to communicate in a way that he can hear what I mean. To me, it's easiest simply to use more direct language with him.

Everyday Clues for Bridging the Communication Gap

The good news for men is that we're not usually expected to respond to our wife's need to talk in any way but to listen. When she finishes talking, she'll feel better — about the world, her problems, herself, and you! So you guys may ask, "How do I know if she wants me to fix something or just to listen?" Well, do what you do best. Be direct! Ask her! When she begins to pour out her heart, ask, "Honey, do you want me to listen, or are you seeking advice?" She'll be glad to tell you!

And wives, remember how clearly your husband understands direct communication. I'll sometimes tell Walt, "I need you to listen like Jennifer, Marian, Kathleen, or Penny."

Even I can understand that!

If I'm working in the office, it helps if Barb simply lets me know when she wants to talk and for how long. She'll say something like, "Hey, honey, would you be free to take a break in about a half hour?" This is brilliant on Barb's part. Giving me a time, a place, and a plan appeals to the design of my brain and makes me feel appreciated. Since my mind systemizes, compartmentalizes, and deals best with one item at a time, the first rule of success when talking to a man, is KISS—Keep It Simple, Sweetheart!

What's my secret for helping Walt listen to me? It's pretty easy:

- *Make an appointment. At breakfast I may say, "Honey, tonight after dinner can we talk about our vacation plans?"*
- *Give him an agenda. I may say, "I want to talk with you about the best time to schedule the repair work on the car."*
- *Let him know there's a time limit. "Would you be able to take a ten-minute break at halftime to chat?"*
- *Let him know whether you want a solution to the topic of your discussion or whether you just want him to listen.*
- *Make sure he has to listen to only one audio input at a time (no children talking, TV blaring, or radio playing).*

If you want to communicate with your husband, don't interrupt when he speaks. Many women don't realize this, but men only interrupt other men when they are being competitive or aggressive.

This can be very difficult for us women because when we're talking with our friends, we talk at the same time about multiple topics. Doing so stimulates our minds, builds our friendships, and strengthens our relationships. My active participation indicates to the other women that I like and accept them. But this does not work when I'm talking with Walt. With women, I speak with my female language; with Walt, I have had to learn to speak in his language.

Finally, women need to understand that when a man does not talk, it is not necessarily a sign that something is wrong. The good news for women is that when your man is silent, there's usually *nothing* wrong with you or your relationship. In fact, giving him the quiet time he needs can strengthen your relationship. When he's ready, he will talk.

As Barb and I have begun to understand the design differences in male and female brains, we've learned how to communicate more effectively. We've discovered what we each need and how we can begin to meet the other's needs. We've learned to appreciate and negotiate around our unique communication methods. Because we've worked on this as a couple, the male/female communication difficulties that can weaken so many marriages have actually helped to make our marriage stronger.

Healthy communication and a good sexual relationship are foundational to every good marriage. We've looked at how differently his brain and her brain communicate; now let's turn our attention to sex and the brain.

PART 3

His Brain,
Her Brain

The Impact
on Relationships

7

Chapter

Sex on the Brain

WHAT IS THE MOST IMPORTANT HUMAN SEX ORGAN? BELIEVE IT OR NOT, it's your brain!

It's probably no surprise to you that when we ask people this question, women usually get the answer correct. What answer do you think men give? You guessed it!

The brain truly is the sexiest organ of them all. It's where the sex drive originates and sexual desires incubate. A man's sex control center in the limbic system, especially the hypothalamus, is much larger than a woman's and is highly sensitive to the hormone, testosterone. Given that men have a larger hypothalamus than women and fifteen to twenty times more circulating testosterone to stimulate their desire for sex, it's no wonder that the male sex drive is so powerful. Women have a lower testosterone level and a smaller hypothalamus, so their sex drive is usually not as strong as a man's.

These fundamental biological differences are just the beginning of many, many ways his brain and her brain function differently when it comes to sex:

- Men tend to be oriented physically; women tend to be oriented emotionally and relationally.
- Men are stimulated by images and sight; women are stimulated by feelings, smell, touch, and words.

- Men can initiate sex anytime and anywhere; women initiate sex less frequently.

- Men are quick to respond sexually and difficult to distract during sex; women are slower to respond and easier to distract.

- Men need orgasm for sexual satisfaction; women do not.

- A man's orgasm is short, intense, physically oriented, and solitary; a woman's orgasm is slower, more intense, emotionally oriented, and (at least potentially) multiple.

Despite these extreme differences, sex is a necessary and highly desirable part of a healthy marriage. When their sexual relationship is healthy, couples have opportunities to give and receive physical pleasure and receive the benefit of an essential emotional and spiritual connection. Sex can build up or diminish closeness, intimacy, and a sense of connectedness. Yet when these differences are not respected and sexual needs are unsatisfied, it can lead to marital conflict. In short, sex is a powerful tie that can bind or tear down; it can "make or break a marital relationship,"[1] especially if men and women don't understand the way his brain and her brain are designed. Dr. Willard Harley has observed, "The typical wife doesn't understand her husband's deep need for sex any more than the typical husband understands his wife's deep need for affection."[2]

Men Are Like Microwaves, Women Are Like Crock-Pots

A man's sex drive can turn on nearly instantaneously. Like cooking in a microwave oven, push the right button, and in seconds the contents are hot, steamy, and ready.

A woman's sex drive is a bit different. The huge connections between her limbic system, emotions, and verbal connections, plus the sensitivity of her skin to touch, her ears to sound, and her nose to aromas, cause her to warm up all over like a Crock-Pot. It may take her longer to heat up, but once she is there, she can cook for quite a long time!

For a man, add a visual image or thought to his ever-ready testosterone, and he's "ready to go." From the onset of sex to orgasm, the average man takes two and a half minutes. For a woman, the average is thirteen minutes.[3]

A woman's sex drive results from a large number of emotional factors, including—but not limited to—closeness, trust, a safe location, the proper touch, a pleasant scent, and the right words, all of which lead to the release of her sex hormones. Her brain and hormones equip her for conversation, holding and hugging, nurturing and bonding. Because of this design, a woman's desire for sex can be dramatically affected by not only the events of her day but also his actions and attitudes toward her during the previous hours, days, weeks, or months.

> *W*omen are wired to respond to what we smell, hear, and feel. So we want a man with soft words, slow hands, and a sexy scent. We want to be softly and gently touched while hearing those "sweet nothings" tenderly and sensitively whispered in our ears.
>
> **Barb Larimore**

Her brain needs time and talk before, during, and after sex. This is because words are all-important to her brain. Language processing is linked deeply and intimately to her emotional center and sex drive. For her, sex usually requires anticipation, preparation, and the right atmosphere—physically and emotionally. A man who understands her need for a soft, slow approach to sex in a safe and quiet environment and seeks to meet these needs will be amply rewarded for his investment.

Whereas she needs words of affection and security spoken before sex, he needs very little discussion. In fact, his brain is so compartmentalized that when he starts having sex, he talks very little, if at all. This lack of talk during sex may cause a woman to think that her husband is not really interested in her—just in sex. The fact is, it's both. During sex, a man uses predominantly his right brain. Functional brain scans during sex (yes, they actually research this) show that "he's so intent on what he is doing that he's virtually deaf."[4] No wonder he doesn't talk!

However, men can respond to some forms of feedback while they are making love: "That feels really good," "Slow down a bit," or a simple "Ooh" or "Ahh." But if you try to start a conversation with him during sex, he'll have to switch from his right brain to the language center in his left brain—and that's like slamming a race car into reverse. Women can successfully multi-task sex and speech, but most men cannot.

Although a man may be nearly deaf during sex, a woman is not. During sex, she can process many auditory inputs from her environment. So while men can have sex almost anywhere—in a room with thin walls, outside, in a room with an open or unlocked door—most women simply do not feel safe or secure in these environments. And if a woman doesn't feel safe, she's going to have problems warming up to sex.

Jim, a new husband I had counseled, learned about this important principle on his honeymoon. After they had returned home, Jim said to me, "Even though we were in a private suite, with the door to the hall locked, she could not make love unless the door from the bedroom to our private sitting room was closed. Even the door from the bedroom to the bathroom had to be shut!" That's female brain chemistry at work!

He Stews, She Sleeps

For a man, sex can be a release and lead to relaxation.

For a woman who is stressed and dog-tired after an eight-hour workday or chasing kids or running errands all day, bedtime is rest time — sleep time.

His sex drive is "up and at 'em!"

She's ready for rest.

He makes his move.

She's not in the mood.

He complains she's nonresponsive and not loving — or worse.

She thinks he's insensitive and not loving — or worse.

He stews and shuts down emotionally.

She sleeps.

Men Respond to What They See, Women Respond to What They Feel

For a woman to ask a man not to notice the shape, curves, and leg length of a good-looking woman is like asking him not to breathe. In many ways, his brain is designed to respond to the shape of an attractive woman in the same way he responds when he sees a fancy computer, a striking car, or an eye-catching flat-screen television.

When a woman sees her man turning his head to gaze at another woman sashaying up the sidewalk, she tends to feel negatively about herself (*I could never look like that. She's much prettier than I am!*), or she thinks negative thoughts about her husband (*You creep, do you prefer her to me?*). Yet, the truth is, any pretty woman will catch a man's attention.

If this happens when Barb and I are walking together, I turn my gaze to her and say, "She's not even in your league, honey."

When Walt does this, it makes me feel safe and secure in our relationship, and it immediately decreases any threat I'm feeling. And I tell him, "I appreciate you not ogling in public."

The fact is, males are stimulated and sexually aroused by what they see—particularly the naked female body. This is part of the reason 76 percent of men want sex with the lights on (while the same is true for only 36 percent of women).[5] It is to a wife's advantage to give him plenty of private opportunities to see her naked so that the images that are burned into his amygdala and hippocampus are hers and hers alone.

A woman, on the other hand, is not usually turned on by seeing her husband naked. It's not that she doesn't want to see him, but the way to her heart is through what she senses and feels, not what she sees. What turns her on is love talk and sentimental feelings. So most women prefer sex with the lights down—and most will close their eyes during sex, as "this perfectly suits a woman's finely tuned sensory equipment."[6]

After sex, the woman's oxytocin surge makes her sensitive to a man's cuddling, nuzzling, whispering, soft touches, and talk. A man who provides his wife with these gifts causes other chemicals to flood her brain—dopamine gives her feelings of well-being, phenylethylamine (PEA) and endorphins increase her feelings of love, and serotonin increases her feelings of emotional security and stability.[7] For many women, feelings of closeness, warmth, safety, intimacy, and affection can be as satisfying as an orgasm.

Having Sex or Making Love, Does It Matter?

Even the way men and women think about sex is different. When a husband thinks about sex with his wife, it usually does *not* include "encumbering relationships, emotional elaboration, complicated plotlines, flirtation, courtship, and extended foreplay."[8] He only imagines the sexual act.

So men, for the most part, can have sex or make love. Both usually result in orgasm for him.

Most women, however, much prefer "making love" to "having sex." Making love means she feels loved and cherished, and being loved and giving love result in the orgasmic rush of chemicals that make her love making love.

But a man doesn't have to love making love. Whether he realizes it or not, he sometimes wants sex just to relieve stress. His brain responds to stress and emotion with a physical response (as opposed to a woman's emotional or verbal response). In the same way, men who are wrestling with a problem or dispute often find that sex relieves the intensity of their conflict and emotion.

The wife in this scenario may feel resentful of having sex—especially before foreplay warms her up. Yet sometimes agreeing to have sex with him is exactly what he needs to work through his problem.

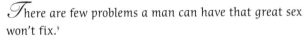

There are few problems a man can have that great sex won't fix.[9]

Barbara and Allan Pease

No matter what the reason, most men think of sex much more often than their wives. In fact, nearly three times as many men as women think of sex at least once every thirty minutes.[10] One national study found that 70 percent of men think about sex every day, which was double the 34 percent rate among women.

Furthermore, 43 percent of men think about sex several times a day, while just 13 percent of women do.[11] Another study found that only 19 percent of women think about sex every day or several times a day—while 14 percent of women think about sex less than once a month.[12]

Tell a man that 67 percent of women think about sex only a few times per month (or at the most a few times per week), and he'll look at you like you have two heads—to him that number just doesn't compute!

> *W*omen want a lot of sex with the man they love, while men want a lot of sex.[13]
>
> **Glen Wilson, PhD**

To desire sex, a man only needs to arrive home and see his wife. But when a wife thinks about sex with her husband, her thoughts are full of "details about the partner and the environment."[14] So it's important for a husband and wife to learn to communicate with each other about their desires and expectations for sex or making love.

For a man to ask a woman to respond sexually, as he does, to images or thoughts is to ask her to do something outside of her design and nature. We wives can give our husbands the recipe to an amazing sex life—but they have to be willing to take time to prepare the meal, set the table, light the candles, and enjoy several courses! If a man tries to dive into the dessert first, he may end up going hungry.

Men Enjoy Sex, Women Enjoy Intimacy

Guys, just because your wife doesn't pursue sex with the same intensity you do, don't make the mistake of thinking she isn't interested in sexual intimacy. One national study found that seven out of ten women said their relationship with their husbands and how their husbands felt about them was on their mind anywhere from "often" to "most of the time."[15] So while he frequently thinks about pursuing sex, she frequently thinks about being pursued. In fact, more than eight out of ten wives report that they would prefer to want to have sex as much as their husbands do (and among happily married women, that desire was almost 100 percent).[16]

However, because her brain has lower levels of the "sexually assertive hormones" than his brain does, she typically has less urge to *pursue* sex than he does. Theresa Crenshaw, MD, writes, "The aggressive sex drive is controlled not just by testosterone, as most people think, but by vasopressin, DHEA, serotonin, dopamine, and LHRH as well. The receptive sex drive ... has been overlooked altogether.... Receptive doesn't necessarily mean passive [but] available, and perhaps willing, but without the initiative to pursue sex."[17]

> *This* doesn't mean she doesn't want [sex], or won't enjoy it once it's happening, but just that seeking it out isn't usually on her mind.[18]
>
> **Jeff and Shaunti Feldhahn**

These facts are important for guys to know, especially if their wives are readers of romance novels (one in three women in the United States are). Most of the guys I talk to have no clue that romance novels constitute 40 percent of all mass-market paperback sales.[19] For those of you who haven't read a romance novel recently (or ever!), the success formula hasn't changed for decades—they create stories of intimacy, romance, and relationship: "It's all love. All the time. Getting love, keeping love, making love."[20]

From A to Almost Z (Minus a Few)

What's the secret to preparing your wife to desire sex with you?[21] Here's a list adapted from authors Barbara and Allan Pease:

Accessorize • acknowledge • anticipate • attend to • brag about • care for • caress • carry for • clothe • compliment • console • cuddle • defend • die for • dream of • embrace • empathize • entertain • excite • fascinate • fix things • forgive • gratify • hug • humor • idolize • indulge • massage • nuzzle • oblige • pacify • pamper • phone • placate • praise • protect • relish • romance • sanctify • savor • serenade • smooch • soothe • spoil • squeeze • stimulate • stroke • support • tantalize • tease • trust • worship.

What's the secret to preparing your husband to desire sex with you?

Arrive naked—with pizza. (Just kidding! The pizza is optional!)

Women usually attach a lot more feelings to sexual intimacy than men do, but there is a time when men find it much easier to get in touch with their feelings about their wife—and it happens to be *after* sex. It's related to the hormone oxytocin—the cuddle hormone that women need to have *before* sex. It turns out that in men the highest levels of oxytocin occur *after* sex. The Peases write, "After a man has had great sex, his softer, feminine side emerges. He can hear birds singing, is struck by the colors of the trees, can smell the flowers, and is touched by the words of a song. Before sex, he probably noticed the birds only because of the mess they made on his car. But a man needs to understand that this after-sex side is the one that a woman loves to see and finds wonderfully seductive."[22]

A wife prefers to see this side of her husband before they make love. Seeing him like this helps her get in the mood to make love. And the more she works with her husband to have great sex, the more often she'll see this side of him.

> *S*adly enough, most affairs start because of lack of affection [for the wife] and lack of sex [for the husband]. She doesn't get enough affection, so she shuts him off sexually. He doesn't get enough sex, so the last thing he feels like being is affectionate.[23]
>
> **Willard F. Harley, PhD**

Meanwhile, men need to learn the art of approaching and pleasing their wives' sexual design. For most men, a slow approach to sex simply does not come naturally. Many of us don't have a clue that our wives are hardwired to respond to "attention, praise, pampering, and lots of time,"[24] as this is how their ovens are designed to heat up!

The fact is, women love to hug. Across most countries and cultures, women hug and love to be hugged.[25] We hug each other; we hug our children; we hug others' children; we hug pets, relatives, and even stuffed animals. Hugging, holding, hearing (listening), and hanging around her are what women say their men most need to do to show affection. Affection goes a long way toward meeting her desire for intimacy. When Walt takes the time to lavish these gifts on me, he builds up an investment in my emotional savings account.

If a man says he's not "the affectionate type" or doesn't like to take the time to hug, hold, and hear his wife but insists that she meet his sexual needs, there will be a problem. He will likely turn off his wife and actually end up meeting neither his nor her needs.

Dr. Willard Harley writes, "When it comes to sex and affection, you can't have one without the other."[26]

Almost all of us men need some tips in how to become more affectionate. In most marriages, our wives are our best instructors—at least if we approach them in the right way. For me, this meant explaining to Barb how much I loved her and confessing how often I failed to express my deep love and care for her appropriately. Then I simply had to ask her to help me learn how she needed me to express affection to her. These are some of the simple actions she suggested I could do to express my love and affection for her:

- *Hug and hold me daily.*
- *Kiss me gently and tell me you love me.*
- *Call me if you are able to break away from your busy schedule to check on me.*
- *Pray daily for my specific needs (and pray with me daily).*
- *Demonstrate your affection for me, in appropriate ways, in front of our children.*
- *Share the high and low points of your day with me so that I can effectively pray for you tomorrow.*
- *Walk in the yard with me, holding my hand.*
- *Enjoy sunsets with me.*
- *Love and spend time with our children.*
- *Join us for dinner—no matter how busy you are.*

The Beast Needs a Beauty

When seeking a lifelong mate, men especially care about how a woman looks—about her beauty. Not only that, the average man's brain is sexually stimulated by visual cues and is built for variety. Although most women know that men are turned on by sexy outfits and lingerie, they have no idea how powerful this is.

Telling men not to become aroused by signs of beauty, youth, and health is like telling them not to experience sugar as sweet.[27]

David M. Buss, PhD

Using functional MRI scans, researchers examined the brains of young men as they looked at pictures of beautiful women. They found that feminine beauty affects a man's brain at a very primal level—similar to what a hungry person gets from a good meal or an addict gets from a fix.[28] One of the researchers said, "This is hard core circuitry. This is not a conditioned response." Another concluded, "Men apparently cannot do anything about their pleasurable feelings [in the presence of beauty]."[29]

As a wife, I want to be the one to provide the variety to which Walt's brain is designed to respond. I don't want him to be tempted to look any farther than me!

Barbara and Allan Pease relate the story of how before every Christmas the lingerie sections of department stores are full of embarrassed men sheepishly walking around trying to find sexy gifts for their wives. They continue with this observation:

> In January, those women are standing in line at the returns counter in the same store. "This is just not me," they say. "He wants me to dress up like a hooker!" The hooker is, however, a professional sex seller who has researched market demands and is packaged to make a sale. One American study has shown that women who wear a variety of erotic lingerie have generally much more faithful men than women who prefer white cotton underwear.[30]

As Walt's wife, I want to look good, not only because it makes me feel good about me, but because I know it's important to Walt. Having an attractive mate is one of a man's most basic needs, and I want Walt to continue to find me attractive.

A wise wife will pay attention to how she looks. Dr. Willard Harley gives two reasons for its importance:

1. When she looks good, he feels good ... most men have a need for an attractive wife. They do not appreciate a woman for her inner qualities alone. They also appreciate the way she looks.[31]
2. You meet an emotional need [for him] by the way you look.... A wife's attractiveness is often a vital ingredient to the success of her marriage, and any wife who ignores this notion—for whatever reason—risks disaster.[32]

The Beauty Needs Romance

For most wives, affection and romance is the cement of their marriages. Affection and romance symbolize security, protection, comfort, and approval—all of which are critical to women.

Dr. Harley writes, "When a husband shows his wife affection, he sends the following messages:

- I'll take care of you and protect you.
- You are important to me, and I don't want anything to happen to you. I'm concerned about the problems you face, and I am with you.
- I think you've done a good job, and I'm so proud of you.

Men need to understand how strongly women need these affirmations. For the typical wife, there can hardly be enough of them."[33]

Romantic displays of affection help build a woman's trust in her husband's love for her. Dr. Steven Rhoads writes, "Sex experts say that for a woman to really enjoy herself [sexually], she must completely relax. Trust in [her] partner would seem essential if the woman is to have a pleasurable experience."[34] So it's no wonder that married women are significantly more likely than cohabiting women to report *emotional* satisfaction with sex.[35] And sex typically gets better and better in the marital relationship. In fact, women say sex is better two years after marriage than it was in the first months.[36]

For cohabiting women, only 7 percent of women who see their sex partners as "relatively short-term propositions" say they are "extremely satisfied physically" with the sex. Even in cohabiting women who expect their relationship to be a long one but not a married one, only 11 percent say the sex is extremely satisfying physically.[37] Put simply, the prospect of a lifetime commitment dramatically boosts sexual satisfaction and frequency among women.[38]

However, a spouse who is unhappy, stressed, or con-flicted—one who is preoccupied, worried, or angry about various (nonsexual) aspects of the relationship—will have a far more difficult time becoming sexually interested in and aroused by the other spouse—particularly if the other person is the source of the conflict or unhappiness.[39]

It is also true that a person who is not satisfied with either the quantity or the quality of sex in the relationship may become dissatisfied with other aspects of the marriage. Whatever the direction of the relationship between sexuality and general satisfaction, most researchers agree that the two are intimately connected. Mutually rewarding sex, along with effective communication about sexual desires and preferences, is clearly associated with sexual satisfaction.[40]

So learning to communicate to your spouse your sexual desires as well as your sexual likes and dislikes can not only increase sexual intimacy but also prevent resentment, bitterness, and anger from building up in your marriage. There is a definite correlation between how happy you both are in the bedroom and how happy you are overall in your marriage.[41]

Happy in the Bedroom?

To spark a discussion about your sexual relationship, here are some questions to get things rolling:

1. What do you really enjoy about our sex life? What pleases you? What feels best and most comfortable for you?

2. What would make it better for you? What would make you feel more comfortable?

3. What's your idea of a "perfect" romantic sexual encounter? What can I do to be more romantic with you?

4. How can I be a better lover? How can I be a better sex partner?

5. When we're together sexually, do you ever feel like a sex object? What makes you feel that way? How can I change that?

6. How do you feel about the frequency of our lovemaking? How can we meet each other's sexual needs, even when our sexual appetites are different?

7. What barriers will we need to overcome for both of us to be satisfied with our sex life? What aspects of our relationship are affecting our sex life? How can we get started in breaking down these barriers?[42]

Is sex critical to a happy marriage relationship? Yes, for both his brain and her brain are designed in such a way that satisfying sex increases the marital bond for a couple. Could this "sex on the brain" that each sex experiences actually be divinely designed? Emphatically, we say, "Yes!" And that's the subject of our next chapter.

8

Chapter

Sex by God's Design

MY FRIEND ROB TOLD ME HE THOUGHT HE WAS DOING A GREAT JOB AS a husband. After all, he worked hard, provided for his wife, and never even considered having an affair. Everyone told Rebecca how fortunate she was to have a good husband like Rob. From the outside, no one could see what was really happening in their marriage.

Rebecca had everything she could possibly want—all bought with Rob's hard-earned money—but she resented Rob's long hours at work. Sometimes she even felt like a single mom. When Rob was home, it was his time to relax. At bedtime he wanted sex, but he never wanted to talk, hold her, or cuddle.

A long time ago he had stopped giving Rebecca hugs and kisses. She couldn't even remember the last time he told her he loved her. "She knows I love her," Rob told me. "I married her, didn't I?"

Over time, Rebecca felt more and more isolated and lonely in her marriage.

Rob resented the fact that Rebecca didn't seem to appreciate his hard work and sacrifice for the family. As his stress levels went up, so did his need for sex, but Rebecca began to refuse him more times than not.

Although there is no abuse or adultery eroding their relationship, Rebecca and Rob's marriage is extremely vulnerable to an affair or to divorce. Their marriage is suffering from Rob's neglect of Rebecca's needs and her refusal to meet his sexual needs. The damage from their dysfunctional physical relationship is subtle and insidious, but it impacts their emotional, spiritual, and marital health. The tragedy is, it is preventable.

Rob and Rebecca have not practiced the biblical principles God designed to help men and women bridge the sexual gap between themselves. Yes, that's right—*biblical* principles!

If Rob would simply learn about and demonstrate on a daily basis the divine design for meeting his wife's sexual needs—and if she would do the same—then their marriage could become stronger and more satisfying than they could imagine. However, if they continue to ignore God's design for their marriage, it could be in real jeopardy.

Is There Sex in the Bible?

Yes, indeed! And *lots* of it!

Our Creator knows all about sex. After all, it's part of his divine design for marriage. It's his gift to us. Because he knows how strong the sex drive he invented can be, he created a relationship in which sex works the very best—the marriage relationship between one man and one woman.[1] Sex in marriage is good and pure;[2] it is intended both for reproduction[3] and for pleasure.[4]

If you have any doubts about how much the Bible has to say about sex, try reading Song of Songs. The entire book is devoted to a delightful and joyful description of the sexual love between a husband and wife. The young husband in the Song of Songs gazes at his young wife and exclaims:

> *You are tall and supple, like the palm tree,*
> *and your full breasts are like sweet clusters of dates.*

I say, "I'm going to climb that palm tree!
  I'm going to caress its fruit!"
Oh yes! Your breasts
  will be clusters of sweet fruit to me,
your breath clean and cool like fresh mint,
  your tongue and lips like the best wine.[5]

Yes, indeed! It's sex, sex, sex! If you read what this book in the Bible says about sex, we promise you'll never think of a garden, palm trees, or love in the same way.

Sex is an amazing gift God has given us to enjoy. After God saw all that he had made, including sex, he declared it to be "very good."[6] God designed his brain and her brain to enjoy each other sexually in marriage.[7] God uses the sexual relationship between a husband and a wife to picture how he relates to and loves his children.[8]

> *God* is the creator of sex and all its pleasures. Orgasm is not some evil, post-fall addition to the process of procreation. It was God who decided that sex should be incredibly enjoyable. He is also the one who established certain parameters (namely, marriage) to protect and maximize the experience.[9]
>
> **Tim and Amy Gardner**

Sex is the physical confirmation of everything that is spiritually joined during the wedding ceremony. The bonding of his brain and her brain that occurs with sex is part of the "cleaving" the Creator describes: "Therefore shall a man leave his father and his mother, and shall cleave unto his wife: and they shall be one flesh."[10] To "cleave" is to be "stuck on," and the most excellent glue that makes a married couple stick to each other is sex—one flesh meant to last a lifetime.

But this incredible gift can also be misused and abused and bring its share of problems. So in all his wisdom, God deemed it necessary to provide us with his divine advice for enjoying sex.

There is tremendous freedom sprinkled with great fun, satisfaction, and enjoyment when these nonnegotiable biblical recommendations are followed within the boundaries of marriage.

Designed for Sex within Marriage

The Creator's fingerprints are on the very physiology of sex. When a man commits to a woman and marries her, his testosterone and androgen levels drop enough that his oxytocin and vasopressin levels lead him to *want* to be in a secure, long-lasting relationship and to find that relationship satisfying. This chemical mixture leads him to want to protect and provide for his wife—to bond with her.

For women, sex in marriage leads to higher oxytocin levels. These increase her feelings of trust while also creating incredibly strong feelings of attachment, comfort, and respect for her husband.

In a monogamous, committed marriage relationship, the man's testosterone surges are blunted and the relationship-building hormones can take over. For men, sex in marriage results in higher levels of oxytocin, which may increase his sperm count, facilitate sperm transport, and strengthen male ejaculation. So marriage may actually lead to greater male fertility.[11] Imagine—all this was designed by God!

Among women, the production of oxytocin varies according to the degree of security in their relationships.[12] The women who have greater security (with fewer negative emotions in their lifetime) experience greater oxytocin production. Researchers have shown that women "who were currently involved in a committed relationship experienced greater oxytocin increases in response to positive emotions than single women." They speculate that "a close, regular relationship may influence the responsiveness of the hormone."[13]

The truth is simple: to love deeply and with greater enthusiasm, we must be highly discriminating about our relationships with the opposite sex. Oxytocin is instrumental in regulating the sex drive in both males and females — it creates a natural feedback loop so that the more sex a couple has, the more they want. Sex with the right person (read husband/wife) produces a psychochemical cocktail that can yield absolute, unconditional and uninhibited love for each other — orgasm causes levels of oxytocin to increase three to five times above normal.[14]

Janice Shaw Crouse, PhD

We have been designed to receive phenomenal rewards for committed monogamous relationships. Researchers have found that during the first eighteen months of marriage, couples have elevated levels of a number of hormones — especially oxytocin — that can be five times the normal level.[15] This "romance cocktail" results in sex being one of the — if not *the* — major activities for a couple during the first few months of marriage. This is no surprise to our Creator; after all, it's part of his "very good" plan.

The chemicals of monogamy are not limited to oxytocin. There is another brain biochemical, dopamine, which appears to ignite intense attraction.[16] Researchers at University College, London, studied men and women who were "truly, deeply and madly" in love with each other. The brains of the volunteers were scanned while they gazed at pictures of either their romantic partners or strangers. When they saw their lovers, their brains lit up in the neural areas that activate during another kind of euphoria that is mediated by dopamine — narcotic addiction.[17]

Clearly God's design is for the marriage of a man and woman to provide neurochemical rewards that increase their satisfaction with each other, with sex, with their relationship, and with their family. It's like divinely designed chemical insurance for marital bliss!

The Secrets of Lifelong Marriage

When a husband and wife have been married and then decide they can't get along, they often use the excuse that they are "incompatible," meaning they are unable to blend or associate because of disharmony. Often they say they are sexually incompatible, when at one time they would have described themselves as "irresistible," or having an overpowering appeal to each other.

However, as marriage therapist Dr. Willard Harley reminds us, "The quickest cure for incompatibility and fastest road to becoming irresistible lie in meeting each other's most important emotional needs."[18] Meeting each other's emotional needs is an essential part of God's design for marriage. Doing so requires unselfish giving and receiving.

> *When* a man agrees to an exclusive relationship with his wife, he depends on her to meet his sexual need. If she fulfills this need, he finds in her a continuing source of intense pleasure, and his love grows stronger. However, if his need goes unmet, quite the opposite happens. He begins to associate her with frustration.... His commitment to [her] has left him with the choice of sexual frustration or infidelity.[19]
>
> **Willard F. Harley, PhD**

A surprise to many couples is that a man cannot achieve sexual fulfillment in his marriage unless his wife is sexually fulfilled as well. For his brain, sex is not just one of a wide variety of options to build a marital relationship. Rather, as Dr. Harley says, "Sex is [for him] like air or water."[20] In an age-old joke, a marriage counselor asks the couple, "How many times a month do you two have sex?" The husband replies, "Hardly ever! Maybe six or seven times." The wife answers, "All the time! Seven, maybe eight, times a month."

This joke points to our different needs and perceptions of what it means to be sexually satisfied, and the research shows similar differences. According to a national survey in the United States, most married couples have sex an average of seven times a month (less than twice a week).[21]

There is tremendous variability in the frequency of sex in marriage, and much of this can be credited or blamed on brain biology and biochemical differences. Some couples have sex very infrequently, whereas others have sex daily. The number of times spouses reported having had sexual intercourse each month during their first year of marriage ranged from one (an average of twelve times that year) to forty-five (or 540 times that first year). However, in most couples, one wants sex more than the other—or one has a higher sexual appetite (libido) than the other. This is usually, but not always, the man.

How is the spouse with the lower libido supposed to respond? The Bible gives us a clue when it teaches, "Marriage is a decision to serve the other, whether *in bed or out*"[22] (emphasis mine). This verse teaches the concept of what Lorraine Pintus calls "the servant lover."[23] This verse is echoed by another: "Be devoted to one another in brotherly love. Honor one another above yourselves."[24] Pintus rephrases these verses this way: "In your sexual relationship, don't let selfishness rule. God asks you to think of your spouse as more important than yourself. So stop thinking about yourself and what you want sexually. Think instead about what your mate desires and how you can please him/her."[25]

When Walt asked me to marry him, he was trusting that I would meet his sexual needs. He was trusting me to be as sexually interested in him as he was in me. He was trusting and believing that I would make myself sexually available to him to meet his needs, just as I trusted him to meet my needs. At times, I must confess that he found a wife unwilling to meet his God-designed needs. Without even realizing it, I was leaving him up the proverbial creek without a paddle. If I had only known then what I know now about being a servant lover.

*S*ervant lovers sacrifice *sexually* for their mates. Servant lovers place their mates' sexual needs above their own and give sexually with selfless abandon. Servant lovers understand the need to give unconditionally, and they acknowledge that this cannot happen unless they learn to surrender their selfish desires.[26]

Lorraine Pintus

Of course, when it comes to sexual desires, some are selfish and potentially damaging to a marriage. The first selfish sexual desire is the spouse who frequently or chronically refuses his or her spouse's sexual needs and advances. Whether this is the husband or wife, the Bible provides this guidance:

The husband should fulfill his marital [sexual] duty to his wife, and likewise the wife to her husband.... Do not deprive each other except by mutual consent and for a time, so that you may devote yourselves to prayer. Then come together again so that Satan will not tempt you because of your lack of self-control.[27]

The *only* reason the Bible gives for refusing to meet your spouse's sexual needs is "by mutual consent" for a limited period of time for "prayer." We both believe that this admonition is for marriages that are fairly healthy. In a marriage where there is physical, verbal, or emotional abuse or significant unresolved conflict, sexual boundaries are not only appropriate but are mandatory. For the vast majority of couples, however, the biblical guidance is clear: say no only rarely.

The second selfish habit is a spouse who insists or demands that all of his or her sexual needs be met day in and day out. We would again point to the verses above to remind this partner that the Bible inspires us to love, serve, and honor our spouse and be willing to sacrifice for our spouse.

The bottom line is this: When his brain and her brain are sexually satisfied, the marriage relationship improves every time. The Creator gave us sex for many reasons, and the fact that he declares that through sex we become "one flesh"[28] hints that sex is a gift that keeps on giving—a gift that strengthens the bonds between a husband and a wife in ways words never could.

Isn't Monogamy Old-Fashioned?

You may be wondering whether the biblical idea of monogamy and sex only in marriage is a bit old-fashioned for our modern times. Not according to much recent research. Sexual frequency and satisfaction are highest for men and women who reserve sex for marriage. Even those who make the mistake of having sex outside of marriage report that sex is still better within marriage. In fact, married women orgasm four to five times more often than women who are single or cohabiting.[29]

One of the most authoritative research projects ever done on sexuality in America was conducted a few years ago at the University of Chicago. This study concluded, "The public image of sex in America bears virtually no relationship to the truth."[30] Contrary to the popular belief that married sex is boring and infrequent, married women and men reported the highest levels of sexual satisfaction. The researchers found that of all sexually active people, married people with only one lifetime partner are most likely to report they are "extremely" or "very" satisfied with the amount of physical and emotional pleasure they experience in their sex lives.[31]

The study's authors believe that the higher level of commitment in marriage is probably the reason for the high level of satisfaction. They explain, "In real life, the unheralded, seldom discussed world of married sex is actually the one that satisfies people the most."[32] In other words, marital commitment contributes to a greater sense of trust and security and more mutual communication between the couple.

Although the science of monogamy is only in its infancy, we predict that researchers will continue to show that God's divine design for marriage is addicting. After nearly thirty-four years of marriage, I'm only beginning to understand to a small degree this design. I've never been more in love or more addicted (in a good sense) to Barb than I am now. To bring to our bedroom hormones and mental pictures that are aroused only by her is a wonderful thing. I can't imagine life without her. No wonder the wedding vows of many of our great-grandparents included this amazing pronouncement:

> With my body, I thee worship. My body will adore you,
> And your body alone will I cherish.
> I will with my body declare your worth.[33]

Being in Love Versus Becoming One

In Louis De Bernieres' novel *Corelli's Mandolin*, an adoring father tries to explain to his daughter what happens when a man's sexual needs and a woman's need for intimacy and affection mesh together in marriage—when they come to understand the difference between "sex" and "love" as compared to "being in love" and "becoming one":

> Love is a temporary madness; it erupts and then subsides. When it subsides, you have to make a decision. You have to work out whether your roots have grown so intertwined that it is inconceivable that you should ever part. Love is not breathlessness; it is not the promulgation of promises of eternal passion. It is not the desire to mate every second of the day, it is not lying awake at night imagining that he is kissing every cranny of your body.... That is being "in love," which any

fool can do. Love itself is what is left over when being in love has burned away. Your mother and I had it; we had roots that grew toward each other underground, and when all the blossoms had fallen from our branches we found that we were one tree, not two.[34]

Any couple can fall in love — and any couple can have sex — which "any fool can do." But love and sex in the marriage relationship, apart from the Creator's design for them, tends to become dull and unsatisfying. True agape love,* practiced by two servant lovers who constantly tend their marriage as they would a precious garden and whose love for their Creator and for each other grows and grows, has the potential to result in a marriage that, like our flower garden, blooms and blooms, resulting in a fragrance of great joy to all who walk in it.

Or as our Creator said, "They will become one flesh"[35] and will have "more and better life than they ever dreamed of"[36] And who wouldn't want that?

---

* We will explain "agape love" in chapter 11.

9
Chapter

His Brain — Conquest;
Her Brain — Nurture

ACCORDING TO THE BIBLE, ADAM, THE FIRST MAN, WAS NOT FORMED in the tame, serene garden of Eden. Rather, he was crafted in the rough-and-tumble wilderness — "born in the outback,"[1] so to speak — before the garden of Eden was created. Maybe that's part of the reason why, when I was a little boy, I felt most at home in the forests and fields surrounding my home. With the other boys, I played the part of soldier, explorer, conqueror, and hero. The specifics of our adventures changed from day to day, but we were always on a quest, always on the lookout for bad guys, always out to build a safer and better world.

I believe the nature of the male brain to conquer and conquest has something to do with why Steven Spielberg's *Saving Private Ryan* is one of my favorite movies. The movie portrays the story of a United States Army Ranger Captain, John Miller, who is assigned to find Private James Francis Ryan, who is not aware that his three brothers have been killed in action. The United States Army wants him found and sent home so his parents don't lose their only remaining son.

One reason this incredible movie is branded into my heart is that it helped me begin to understand a bit of what my father must have experienced fighting in Europe with the army during World

War II. The second reason the movie made such an impression is that it played so well to my masculine brain's design and traits. The movie embodied sacrifice and honor, surrender of self and courage, respect of country and love of family.

As the movie draws to a close, Captain Miller is wounded and dying on a bridge in a French town. Private Ryan kneels down beside him, and Captain Miller utters his last words to the man he gave his life to save: "James, earn this. Earn it!" The camera focuses on the face of the young Private Ryan and then morphs to the face of the elderly James Ryan, who is standing over Captain Miller's grave.

The elder Ryan's lips quiver and his eyes fill with tears. He speaks to the gravestone: "To be honest with you, I wasn't sure how I'd feel coming back here. Every day I think about what you said to me that day on the bridge. I've tried to live my life the best I could. I hope that was enough."

Ryan's wife walks up to him, and he says to her, "Tell me I have led a good life. Tell me I'm a good man." His wife, deeply touched by her husband's display of emotion, softly and empathetically replies, "You are."

> The life of a man — various, complex, irreducible — begins in the male brain's drive to prove worth against all wounding, all hardship, all challenge ... boys and men make a lifelong, nature-based search for self-worth, ... [which] is very different from a girl's or woman's.[2]
>
> **Michael Gurian**

What causes my deepest emotions to rise to the surface when I see this movie? I think it is because of the way God designed and created me as a man. It's because of the male brain's hardwiring and hormonal blueprint. God designed men to prevail, overcome, and conquer. We understand in our gut what is written on our hearts — that we must make something of ourselves and our lives. Deep down we know (and have known since we were little boys) that we were created for adventure and conquest—for a great cause, a mighty quest.

Unlike Adam, Eve was fashioned in the lush, fragrant beauty of the garden of Eden—in its safe, secure shelter. God designed a woman's brain to be verbal, relational, and nurturing. So it should be no surprise that the female impulse—even at a very young age—is to be at home and make a house a home. This helps explain why I, like most little girls, felt so at home talking with my girlfriends about what it would be like to be married and have a family. We could spend hours talking about the kind of man we hoped to marry, dreaming of what our wedding and honeymoon would be like, and imagining what it would be like to have children—in short, having a husband to love and care for me and having a family to nurture.

It also helps explain why one of my favorite movies is You've Got Mail, *a romantic comedy that features New Yorkers Kathleen Kelly and Joe Fox. They meet online and begin to correspond by email. They reveal their personal hopes and dreams and share their favorite books and movies, but they have never connected in real life, even though they live in the same neighborhood, buy their coffee at the same Starbucks, and frequently pass each other on the street.*

Early in the movie, I'm hooked on how Joe opens his heart to Kathleen. She and I both have brains that respond to the oxytocin surge of his romantic emails. We, like most women, are created to desire a husband for life who loves and romances us, and we desire to raise and nurture children with him. Part of me just can't wait for them to meet face-to-face and fall in love, but the reality is that if Kathleen and Joe were to meet, their individual professional objectives, if revealed to each other, would sink their budding romance. You see, Kathleen runs a lovely little children's bookstore, The Shop Around the Corner, while Joe is the heir of Fox Books, a predatory bookstore conglomerate that eventually puts Kathleen out of business.

After Kathleen is forced to close her store, she's at home, depressed, and has a cold. Joe (whom she has met but doesn't know is her email buddy, who goes by the moniker "NY 152") drops by and brings her favorite flowers—daisies. Just before he leaves, she asks, "Why did you stop by?"

"I wanted to be your friend," Joe responds. "I knew it wasn't possible. What can I say? Sometimes a person just wants the impossible."

In the final scene, Kathleen walks down a path in the park for her "first" meeting with "NY 152." She still does not know that Joe, her professional enemy, is "NY 152," her email romance. She stops and looks around. A young woman who is jogging passes by. Kathleen looks at her watch, then hears a dog barking. Joe's dog, Brinkley, charges around the corner. She looks up, sees Joe, and starts to cry. By this time, tears are flowing down my face as Joe walks up to her, puts his arms around her, and says, "Don't cry, Shopgirl, don't cry."

Just before they kiss, she looks up at him and says, "I wanted it to be you. I wanted it to be you so badly."

This movie struck a chord deep in my soul—as it has in every woman I know who has seen it. Every time I see it, I cry. Why do women have this emotional response to romantic movies? It comes from the way our Creator designed the female brain's hardwiring and our hormonal blueprint. There's no escaping the truth that we are designed to build and nurture relationships. Deep down we know (and have since we were little girls) that we were created for love and to be loved—to be a wife and a mom.

There's No Escaping Our Differences

The male drive for conquest and the female drive for nurture are innate. These drives originate in our divine design and are orchestrated by the vastly different interaction of our hormones, reproductive systems, and brains. If we don't recognize and respect these differences, they can result in a lot of conflict and confusion.

Women may view men as insensitive because they are less empathetic and compassionate, or as louts because they don't love *You've Got Mail* and other wonderful movies. And men may view women as weak or soft because they have less desire to compete and be aggressive, or because they don't love movies like *Saving Private Ryan.*

However, just because we are different doesn't mean that men don't nurture or that women aren't powerful. We simply do these things to different degrees and in different ways. Males can be very nurturing, but they tend to relate "through aggression" rather than through "empathy nurturance."[3]

> *A* woman is biologically hardwired to nurture, provide comfort and seek social support in times of stress.... Men have [the tend-and-befriend] instinct too, but to a lesser degree because of hormone differences.[4]
>
> **Shelley E. Taylor, PhD**

For example, a woman will hold and cuddle a baby, while a man will playfully swing a baby into the air. And most babies are delighted by both types of interaction—cooing with delight at a woman's cuddling and squealing with glee at a man's rough-and-tumble excitement.

Men use dominance and aggression for winning and achieving status, and women exert a much more refined and subtle power. As the psychological studies have shown again and again, women are far better than men at sensing, understanding, and predicting the behavior of others. They can "sense the motives behind speech and behavior."[5] So a woman's innate ability to read men better than men can read her empowers her in a unique way.

I think of a man's power being like the motor of the car—he can make it go fast. But a woman's power is like the steering wheel and the brakes—essential parts that lead to safe travel. The two together make a long, satisfying journey possible.

Walt Larimore, MD

Walt's right. When I think of the strength of a woman's power, I immediately think of the scene in the movie My Big Fat Greek Wedding *where Toula, the engaged daughter, is talking with her mother, Maria. Maria dispenses wise marital wisdom when she says, "The man may be the head of the family, but the wife is the neck, and she can turn the head in whatever direction she wants." A woman's unique power comes from her strengths in creating relationships by bonding and building families and friends—and, as a result, building the foundation of a healthy culture and society.*

So instead of "bumping heads" about these seemingly conflicting differences, let's see if we can better understand and appreciate them. After all, the biologic basis of these differences is well documented.

His Brain Designed to Conquer

Many studies have shown that a man's aggressive behavior is linked to two neurohormones. The first is testosterone—associated with impulsivity and spontaneous aggression—and the second is serotonin. When compared to women, men have more testosterone and less serotonin, especially in the decision-making frontal cortex.[6]

In addition, functional brain scans of the areas of the limbic system associated with aggression show greater activity in men than in women. Women, in contrast, have greater activity in the cingulate gyrus area of the limbic system, which is associated with reduced aggression.[7] From an anatomical perspective, the orbital frontal cortices of the brain, which are associated with aggressive behavior, are much larger in men than women. Furthermore, this area of the brain is believed to be impacted by the testosterone wash that occurs in the uterus, as well as by the lack of the calming effects of serotonin.[8]

These biologic differences are critical for women to understand because boys, and the men they grow up to be, have brains that are built to be more aggressive, more impulsive, and more assertive—their design is to earn their self-worth. They are compelled to discover their calling and meaning in life. They are made to conquer the world around them, and they begin their conquests at a surprisingly early age. For instance, my mother told me that I, as a fearless tot, would run away from her and toward any perceived adventure as soon as I could walk.

And my behavior, I must add, was perfectly normal for a boy. By six months of age, boys are far less fearful than girls, and "fearlessness" is associated with levels of testosterone (the higher the level of testosterone, the higher the level of "fearlessness");[9] by thirteen months, boys are demonstrably more aggressive and assertive than girls;[10] and by thirty-six months, boys dominate mixed-gender groups of children. By the time they are in preschool, boys demonstrate far more interest in "rough-and-tumble play" than girls and have no reservations about fighting or destroying things.[11]

Although a woman's natural tendency may be to assume that such behavior is harmful, it was critical for me as a mother to learn that this type of play is actually essential to a boy's healthy development. When boys engage in rough-and-tumble play, they actually are learning to manage their aggression and to discern how competitive they can be.[12] It was especially important for me to know that Walt and Scott's rough play together, like that between most boys and their fathers, is more likely to teach self-control than aggression.[13]

I also learned that even during their preschool years, boys begin to demonstrate a behavior that most of them continue through-out life—they won't listen when girls give them instructions![14] This aspect of the male drive to conquer the world became obvi-ous to me one afternoon when Scott was only five years old.

I received a frantic call from my neighbor Edna. "Barb!" she shouted into the phone. "Get over here! Scott's up on my roof!"

I ran across the street and there he was, walking the roofline of Edna's house. Edna was squawking at him: "Scott, you come down now! You might get hurt!"

Looking at her incredulously, Scott replied, "Well, I might not!" There was my son on a great adventure, wearing only shorts and cowboy boots, certain that he didn't need the advice of a woman!

> Men want to fight the good fight.... Boys start from a very young age with the quest.... The male impulse (is) to be heroic; to be the best ... thus making life into a risk-filled, success/failure, win/lose quest for worth and power.[15]
>
> **Michael Gurian**

One study of fourth- and sixth-grade boys found that at play-time, boys were competitive with other boys over 50 percent of the time, while girls were competitive with other girls only 1 percent of the time.[16] When researchers let children play with big plastic cars that they can drive, they find that more little boys play the "ramming" game. They deliberately drive the vehicle into another vehicle or another child.[17] Their testosterone and vasopressin kick in, and aggression and competition rule. It is also why teenage boys will, not infrequently, participate in very risky behavior. It is part of their search for their calling, part of their hope for dem-onstrating their masculinity and finding meaning.

There is, indeed, something "fierce in the heart of every man."[18] Every man is designed to participate in a quest—to be

a hero, to conquer, to compete. Counselor and author John Eldredge notes, "Capes and swords, camouflage, bandanas and six-
shooters—these are the uniforms of boyhood. Little boys yearn
to know they are powerful, they are dangerous, they are someone
to be reckoned with." And Eldredge is "convinced these desires
are universal, a clue into masculinity itself. They may be mis-
placed, forgotten, or misdirected, but in the heart of every man is
a desperate desire for a battle to fight, an adventure to live, and
a beauty to rescue."[19]

A man's biological tendency toward aggression coupled with
his inborn drive to earn his way results in a deep-seated "notion
of legacy."[20] Like the aged Private Ryan, we men want to know,
"Have I done it? Have I led a good life? Have I been a good man?"
And there are two people on earth from whom we need to hear
this affirmation louder than any other—other men (particularly
our fathers) and our wives.

First of all, along the path of proving their worth, men need
the affirmation of other men. And no male affirmation is more
important than that which a boy or man receives (especially
early in his life) from his father. Remember what happened when
Jesus came up out of the Jordan River after having been baptized
by John? His Father looked down and said, "This is my Son,
whom I love; with him I am well pleased."[21] Whoa—those are
the words every man wants to hear! That's an affirmation from
the Father of all fathers! It's an affirmation for which all men are
designed—and it's written on our hearts by our Creator.

This same Father declares to those with whom he has a personal relationship that we are his children: "To all who received
him, to those who believed in his name, he gave the right to become children of God—children born not of natural descent,
nor of human decision or a husband's will, but born of God."[22]
He thinks about you, delights in you, and rejoices over you and
sings to you;[23] his angels rejoice over you,[24] and you are the object
of his affection.[25] He loves you with every speck of his enormous

love. No matter how much he loves others, he cannot possibly love anyone else more than he loves you. And although it's hard for our minds to fathom, God loves you just as much as he loves Jesus.[26] Now *that's* affirmation!

The affirmation we long for can be found in all its fullness only in our heavenly Father. We are fully loved, fully accepted, by a Father who simply will *never* let us go.[27] And it is from this spring of endless love and affirmation that we as husbands and fathers can sacrificially and selflessly love our wives and children.

Second, every man also wants to be a hero to and rescuer of his true love—it's a trait engraved deep into our brains and hearts by God, who is the hero and rescuer of *our* souls.[28] That's part of the power in Nehemiah's call to his men to defend Jerusalem: "Don't be afraid of them. Remember the Lord, who is great and awesome, and fight for your brothers, your sons and your daughters, your wives and your homes."[29]

But no matter how much men love their wives and their children, the home is not the primary proving grounds on which a man must carry out his drive for accomplishment. For wives and mothers to begin to understand that their husbands and sons are built for quest and conquest, that their design is to seek to measure and compare their self-worth with other boys and men, can be a revelation. Men will make great sacrifices in this quest, and if they ever lose their calling or their path toward conquest, they tend to become withdrawn, depressed, and demotivated.

Her Brain Designed to Nurture

The sex differences in nurturing appear at even earlier ages than the differences in the drive for conquest. These differences occur well before girls and boys are capable of reliably discriminating between the genders or knowing which behaviors are more characteristic of one than the other.[30] Even among children ages twelve months to twenty months, exposure to the distress of other people causes girls to respond with more empathy and less indifference than boys.[31]

These differences only increase as girls grow older. No matter what their age, girls are more cooperative and boys are more competitive.[32] School-age girls try to reduce conflict, while their male classmates seem to revel in it.[33] Her brain wants to network and nurture; his brain wants clash and combat. And after puberty, when, as one researcher puts it, "the soothing effects of estrogen are fully available,"[34] there is an even more marked increase in the female preference for cooperation.[35]

In fact, researchers have found that a woman's desire for "harmonious connections is highly associated with estrogen,"[36] so when levels of the hormone estrogen begin to rise, the female superiority in nurturing and cultivating relationships becomes even more dramatic.[37] And the urge to nurture becomes even stronger under the influence of the hormones oxytocin and prolactin, which are released in large quantities during pregnancy and breastfeeding.[38]

Theresa Crenshaw, MD, believes women are peacemakers and nurturers because of their hormonal makeup — "relatively high levels of serotonin compared to the male, oxytocin in abundant supply, and estrogen, a gentle, ordinarily soothing antidepressant hormone."[39] Steven E. Rhoads, PhD, observes, "Another reason women are the peacemakers is their deep need for amiable connection. And their most important connections are at home. Women say that family relationships are the key to their happiness. Family distress has more effect on the mental health of wives than of husbands."[40]

In both males and females, oxytocin promotes bonding and a calm, relaxed emotional state. In men it is released in large quantities during orgasm. In women, various stimuli, even the act of stroking her baby,[41] can prompt a release of oxytocin. A natural opiate, oxytocin causes women to feel "euphoric" or "exhilarated" while nursing.[42] God designed the female brain to receive the full impact of oxytocin. Not only do women have more receptors in the brain for oxytocin than men, but the number of receptors for oxytocin increases during pregnancy![43]

The fact that women are better at nurturing than men is no surprise to the vast majority of people. A national survey found that 87 percent of men and 78 percent of women believe that women are biologically better suited to nurture and care for children.[44] Multiple studies have concluded that women are "more empathetic, tender-minded, and nurturing than men."[45]

It is important to realize that nurturing has a remarkably positive effect on women. Being able to nurture children in the home is "associated with better health for women."[46] Ninety-three percent of mothers think their children are a source of happiness all or most of the time, while 86 percent of mothers with children under age eighteen say their relationship to their children is crucial to their personal happiness (rating it ten on a ten-point scale).[47]

Alice McDermott, an award-winning novelist, described how she and her female friends in graduate school were transformed by becoming mothers. She says, "The joy of children seemed … too satisfying, too marvelous" to be put in words. But she asked her friends to try. They said things like, "Becoming a mother is the best thing I've ever done." "It's like floating in warm milk." "I could fill a stadium with babies."[48]

In addition to the inborn desire to care for and nurture their children, women enjoy the fact that children respond more favorably to their care. Although children seem to have no preferences whether they play with Mom or Dad, they have an overwhelming preference for being comforted by their mothers. All in all, when babies and toddlers have a preference, they prefer their mother's caring to their father's by fourteen to one.[49]

The desire to nurture and the benefits of nurturing aren't limited to married women who have children. It is well established that daughters are more likely to care for sick parents than sons[50] and that women are more likely than men to care for the family pet.[51] Single women of all ages not only seek outlets for nurturing but can become healthier by nurturing. For example, single women who care for a pet can have significant reductions in their blood pressure.[52]

It's not social conditioning that explains the unadulterated joy and satisfaction a woman gains in nurturing—it's designed into her brain. No wonder they have so much anguish and agony when they are childless or lose a child. Women undergoing infertility treatments have levels of depression comparable to patients with AIDS and cancer.[53] For women who have had a miscarriage, the risk of a major depression within six months is five times higher.[54]

Walt and I lost four children to miscarriage. The pain of each loss for me was exponentially higher than the one before. Walt cried and hurt with each loss—but my distress was worse than torture. Part of my soul was ripped from me, and the loss of those children still leaves a vacuum in my heart.

Conquest and Nurture Happily Ever After

So is it possible for conquest and nurture to live happily ever after? Absolutely! That is exactly what God intended, and it is possible through what W. Bradford Wilcox, PhD, calls "soft patriarchs" or "servant leaders." In his research, he has found that these are the type of men who attend to their wives' needs for

Studies all over the world indicate that women … select, for romantic relationships and marriage, the men who are on a quest for achievement and status. Women want men who aspire to be kings (even if only at a local level), warriors (protectors who make them feel safe), magicians (men who have, even if in a love of gadgets, some magical power that leads to success), lovers (men who make women part of their quest).[55]

Michael Gurian

communication and affection and also are aware of their responsibility to meet their family's financial needs and to provide moral leadership. These types of men are more likely to be directed and informed by the Bible and its model of marriage. They are also more likely to understand that there is a "sacred obligation to use their familial power to serve their families."[56]

A woman's desires for a strong man fit perfectly with the hero mentality that "is biologically wired into men's minds."[57] And scientific studies support this. One review of over twenty studies on marital happiness concluded that wife-dominant couples were the least happy and that wives in the wife-dominated unions were less happy than their husbands. In other words, marriages seem to work best when "the wife can influence the husband" but doesn't try to dominate or disrespect him.[58]

> *If* marriage means bringing together one person built for conquest and assertion and another with a penchant for nurture and loving, we should not be surprised to find that the former is, in some sense, the head of the family.... This doesn't mean he rules like an absolute dictator. Indeed, it's still quite common to hear of small, feminine women who have their strong, masculine husbands "wrapped around their little fingers." Happy women usually rule indirectly. They can rule because their husbands love and want to please them.... In such cases, both parties emerge happy.[59]
>
> **Steven E. Rhoads, PhD**

Most males simply are not attracted to women who try to control them.[60] Studies show that men "positively dislike" dominant tendencies in a female mate.[61] Why? It goes back to a male brain's biologic design to conquer. When he is successful, "he achieves a pleasurable testosterone high; when he fails, loses, or is demeaned, he experiences a testosterone low."[62]

Although a woman seems to be built to desire a man who leads her, she also needs a man who values and honors her — who is loyal to her and respects her. Male dominance is good for a marriage when it is "moderate, not autocratic."[63] So while women are attracted to strong, masculine men, they do not want a man who is tyrannical. In fact, women regularly divorce men who behave like ruthless dictators and who devalue them.[64]

Honoring Each Other's Design

His brain is designed to evaluate and understand things, people, and systems and their relationship to other things. His brain is activated by and designed for doing and fixing—as opposed to her brain, which is created to link emotions and words, friends and friendships, care and caring. No wonder men define themselves by their work and accomplishments—what they accomplish, fix, and solve—and women by their affiliations and associations—who they care for.

Women, because of their large and active verbal centers, the strong connections between their verbal and emotional systems, and estrogen- and oxytocin-driven yearnings to nurture and network, are hardwired for relationships—and they define themselves by the quality of their relationships. In addition, her brain is created with a God-designed search to be desired and pursued, to have an adventure to share with her hero, and to have her true inner beauty recognized and unveiled.

Walt may long for battles to fight, but most of all, I want him to fight for me. The feminine heart wants to be fought for, cherished, and honored. No wonder, as little girls, we are naturally drawn to stories where the knight rescues the kidnapped princess, where the soldier storms the walls to liberate the captive lady, where the swashbuckling seaman sets free the damsel in distress.

While Walt may need a great adventure to tackle to satisfy how he was designed, I also need to be part of something greater than myself. Of course, I recognize that to build a family, to bear and nurture our children, is to participate in something far greater than myself. But there is something more. Although I want and need security, safety, and some degree of stability, I also need to know that I am an essential part of his adventure. I don't necessarily need to be on the trail, aboard the ship, or in the wilderness—but I want to be included.

Walt may need a beauty to rescue, but I have a seductive and hidden side that needs to be unveiled. As a little girl, I delighted in my father's approval and affection. As a teen, I wanted to enchant a young man. As a wife, I need to know I have my husband's heart and attract his eyes—and only he can assure me that I'm doing just that.

Walt and I experienced a crisis as we neared the end of writing this book. The deadline was looming, and we had an enormous amount of work to do. With just forty-eight hours left, a wedding to attend, and a very dear relative just hospitalized for a possible stroke, Walt and I found ourselves laboring in different rooms. I brought four chapters down to his office, but I had not understood exactly what he needed me to do. He snapped, and I snapped right back. Our words to each other were harsh and hurtful. I fled to the safety of the kitchen and cried.

After a bit, Walt came to me and pulled me into his arms. He told me that no book or timetable was more important than me. He would stop writing the book and return the advance to the publisher rather than lose me. He would not be part of curdling my heart just to complete a book.

Walt could have told me to get tough. He could have tried to coach me to finish strong. He could have tried to exhort me to stand firm. He did none of these masculine things. Instead, he prized and protected my feminine heart. He wisely recaptured me rather than wounding or scarring me.

Of course, a wife must honor her husband's brain design as well. A wise wife will recognize the wisdom in the advice of marriage therapist Michael Gurian: "You may notice it gives him pleasure and pride to review his accomplishments and potentials.... As he provides you with details ... a beautiful and mysterious thing is going on: he is bonding with you through the presentation of himself to you."[65]

If he has done nothing heroic on a given day—or in a given week—he may well feel like a failure, and he might try to overcome this feeling by living vicariously through the accomplishments of his favorite sports star ... [or] some kind of competition. Even if he does this in a poker game ..., he'll probably feel better, feel that he has, after all, overcome a challenge—acted heroically, with freedom and power.[66]

Michael Gurian

A wise wife will also recognize that a male's way of thinking may have potential blind spots. He often does not fully process thoughts or emotions before acting. He does not always see all the potential risks or consequences. And many times he does not realize his own power—the strength of his actions and particularly his words. Yet he's designed to respond to a wife who loves him and respects him enough to say, "I don't think you saw it, but you really hurt our son/daughter/friend when you did ... [or when you said ...]."

For example, after Scott, our son, finished mowing and weedeating our lawn one afternoon, he asked his dad to come out and see if the job was complete—because successfully finishing his chore was a condition for leaving for a school event. Walt and he went outside. Before long, Scott came inside angry and in tears. As I comforted him, he vented to me that his dad never approved of anything that he did—it was never good enough. "Dad always finds something wrong."

I realized that Walt just wanted his son to do his chores in an excellent manner. However, he could improve on the way he was communicating with Scott. That evening, we took a walk in the yard. I told Walt, "Did you know how hurt Scott was after you inspected his work this afternoon?"

Walt looked me incredulously. "No! He was hurt? Why?" he asked.

I explained, "I didn't think you had recognized it. Walt, Scott really needs your encouragement and affirmation. He wants to do a good job for you and gain your approval, but you hurt him with the way you provide feedback." I was quiet for a moment to give him time to process what I had said. I could see that he was receiving my message without being defensive, and I knew I was communicating effectively with him. We went on to have a wonderful talk about how Walt could improve his feedback. The next week, after Scott had completed his yard duties, both father and son came in laughing. Scott gave me a thumbs-up, and I knew his father had done better.

Barb understood that a man is built not only to conquer but also to be admired. She made her appeal to me by showing both how I had hurt and discouraged my son and how I could do better. We truly are better together than apart!

10
Chapter

His Brain — Provision;
Her Brain — Security

As Barb and I were writing this chapter, we took a break to see *Little Shop of Horrors*, a play that is a campy throwback to the 1950s. Having seen the musical before, I was interested in the response of the audience. When Audrey, one of the lead characters, began to sing about her dreams of getting married and escaping Skid Row, I looked around at the college-aged audience — predominantly made up of young females — expecting a response of laughter or revolt. I thought I knew what was coming, but was I ever surprised!

Initially, I saw smiling faces all around as Audrey began to sing of her desire for a small matchbox home — with a barbecue grill on the patio and a stylish backyard fence. However, when Audrey chanted on about her dream of keeping the house neat and clean while her husband did the outdoor chores, I saw the faces of some of the younger women turn a bit taut.

"They're gonna go crazy!" I thought, as Audrey continued to croon about cooking a frozen dinner for her husband and together watching their favorite comedy show on their colossal twelve-inch TV screen. I heard laughter ripple across the crowd as they conjured up thoughts of their own big-screen TVs. But I also saw tears — lots of tears. I was stunned by their response as

Audrey finished her solo about the home she envisioned as being not only located far from her Skid Row but featured in *Better Homes and Gardens.*

The crowd, most of whom I assumed would erupt in anger or resentment if anyone dared to utter such sentiments in everyday conversation, thundered their applause. I was amazed at how they embraced a theatrical character who so clearly verbalized the divinely designed needs and desires that are hardwired deep within each of us.

Although such thoughts of a traditional home and marriage seem unpopular among many who wish to direct our cultural values, they accurately reflect the differences between his brain and her brain when it comes to provision and security—she longs for the security that comes as he provides materially for the family and protects her.

Most of us guys, unless we've been living on another planet or are totally oblivious to women, know that women desire security. And most women recognize that men desire deeply to protect and provide for their wives and families. By now it shouldn't surprise you to learn that these divinely designed differences are partially manifested in our brain chemistry.

Brain Chemistry and Happiness at Home

One of the most profound biological differences between male and female brain chemistry lies in a woman's high levels of oxytocin, which focus her brain on finding bonding opportunities while nurturing relationships.

Although women can achieve bonding outside of the home, their highest levels of oxytocin occur when they are secure in a happy marriage that enables them to create a comfortable home where they can birth, nurse, and nurture their children. Oxytocin pulls them toward the permanence of attachment, making a home, and raising a family.[1] So when women seek a lifelong mate, they want, of course, a spouse who is considerate, honest, interesting, and loyal.[2] But they also almost universally seek men who can support and provide for them.[3] A good provider is important to them because, when given the choice, most women receive their greatest satisfaction and contentment from homemaking and child rearing. Even if they work outside the home, women still take homemaking very seriously[4] and may even feel cheated if their husbands take over what women consider to be their homemaking responsibilities.[5]

How does a woman's inborn need to create a home affect a marriage? Consider something as seemingly simple as washing dishes. Barb and I see glassware completely differently. To me, it's clean if most of the food and grime is rinsed off. To Barb, it's not clean until it shines. There are biological reasons behind this, because men and women literally see things very differently. As a male, I have a much less perceptive eye for detail than does Barb. But perhaps the more important factor is that a crystal-clean glass is a much lower priority to me than to Barb.

> *To* a woman, where the home is less of a motel, and more the backdrop to the relationships that matter to her, the dirty glass stands as an implicit rebuke to her own values.... It matters to women whether or not their homes are pleasant and hygienic places to be in, because what matters to women — love, affection, relationships, security — takes place in the home.[6]
>
> **Anne Moir, PhD**

The truth is, most of my guy friends find that their wives do most, if not all, of the indoor home cleaning because most men do such a crummy job of it. One friend told me, "Earlier in our marriage, I did everything I could to help out around the home. But her standards for clean are a whole lot higher than mine. I'd like to help out more — to do more — but she makes me feel inadequate. She says that if I do something in the house, she'll just have to do it all over again. That makes me feel pretty rotten. So when she cleans the house, I go work in the yard." Another husband says, "I no longer claim to 'clean' the house. Instead, I 'improve' it. When my wife is overloaded, she can appreciate my efforts to improve things, but we both know it's not anywhere near her definition of clean."

Walt and I have had to learn to deal with these fundamental differences in brain chemistry and perceptions as well. Whenever I'm feeling down or sick, he'll often—and with the best intentions—try to take up the slack by doing some of the household chores I normally do. But no matter how hard he tries, his efforts often fail to provide the relief he desires to give me. One reason is because I actually get therapeutic pleasure from doing those chores; the second is because I want them done the way I do them.

I have learned that Dr. Anne Moir is absolutely right when she explains that when husbands get "into trouble by misstacking the dishwasher, in however trivial a manner, or misfolding the tablecloth; the hormones are accentuating a basic sex difference in attitudes and perceptions."[7]

But what about the other side of the coin? Do a man's hormones affect the male drive to provide and protect and a woman's desire for security? You bet they do. We think you'll be amazed to see how these divinely designed needs for provision and security work together.

Men, of course, are less dominated by oxytocin and more dominated by testosterone and vasopressin. These hormones push them toward aggressive persistence in proving themselves to their wives and the world rather than staying home and caring for children. Their testosterone- and vasopressin-driven independence and their emotional need to be admired and respected by others drive them to leave the home and seek their place in the world. They do this to provide for their wives and to make them happy.[8] So being successful in providing for their wives is very important—even essential—to their feelings of self-worth.

Yet many husbands and wives don't realize how deep and powerful a man's biological need to be recognized and admired for successfully providing for his wife and family really is. Providing for a wife and family is like an inborn biological "test" in which every man wants to excel. This desire to excel in providing for his family is exactly what God has designed men to do and women to need and appreciate.

I love the way Barbara and Allan Pease describe how our biological design and needs complement each other: "A man's biological urge is to provide for a woman, and her appreciation of his efforts confirms his success. If she is happy, he feels fulfilled. If she is not happy, he feels that he is a failure because he believes he can't provide enough." They go on to say, "He needs to be told by a woman that he is successful at what he does and that what he can provide is fine."[9] For our husbands, providing for us and protecting us is built into their DNA. If we try to usurp or minimize what our husband is built and designed to do, we put our marriage in peril.

Barb is right. Our marriages are in peril if we ignore God's design in this area. Consider the following documented outcomes when provision and security are out of balance in marriage:

- Women divorce men who are not ambitious and do not work steadily at good jobs.[10]
- A husband rarely feels good when his wife supports him financially.[11]
- Couples with ambitious wives or those who have increasing income are more likely to divorce.[12]
- Young, highly educated, and occupationally successful fathers in dual-career marriages are less satisfied with their work, marriages, and personal lives than similar men who are sole providers.[13]

- When both spouses work, couples report that it is "easier for the marriage" when the wife's career is "less [financially] successful than her husband's." Most women hold this view because (1) they believe the husband's work is more important to "his sense of self," and (2) they need their husband to be successful.[14]

- Couples will go to great lengths to conceal a high-earning wife's income to protect the husband's status as primary provider.[15]

> *D*ivorce rates are far higher when the wife's career is more successful than the husband's. Why? Neither the newly liberated alpha women nor their shell-shocked beta spouses seem comfortable with the role reversal.... First, the wife starts to lose respect for her husband, then he begins to feel emasculated, and then sex dwindles to a full stop.[16]
>
> **Ralph Gardner Jr.**

These observations are not merely about "role reversal." They are neither sexist nor chauvinistic. Rather, they are about ignoring our innate design and snubbing our noses at our Creator's plan and intention. No wonder the Bible condemns men who do not provide for their families: "If anyone does not provide for his relatives, and especially for his immediate family, he has denied the faith and is worse than an unbeliever."[17] The manner of provision has a tremendous impact on the health of a marriage and family. Research by Dr. Steven Rhoads leads him to conclude that "married men usually take well to the provider role ... work caters to a part of men's nature. It allows them to roam beyond the family fire. It provides a competitive outlet. A salary gives a tangible indicator of progress."[18] He goes on to say, "Women like to care for children much more than men do, and they also like housework more than men do.... There is strong reason to think that such differences have a biologic basis."[19]

When Wives Work Outside the Home

So what's a couple living in a society where dual incomes are increasingly the norm to do? Is it wrong for married women to work outside the home? Is it possible to provide for a family while honoring our divinely designed differences? Barb and I answer with an emphatic "No!" to the first question and "Yes" to the second. We do not disapprove of any woman who wants a career, but we believe it is essential that we provide for our families in a way that honors God's design and maximally nurtures children. So how can we do this successfully?

> *Time* after time I've been told by married women that they resent having to work. The women I talk to usually want a choice between following a career and being a homemaker — or possibly they want a combination of the two. . . . I wish, rather, to stress the principle that many women need to have the *choice* of whether or not to work once they have children. If they do choose a career, the money they earn should not have to be spent on basic support of the family.[20] . . . I've been amazed by the number of women who feel much better toward their husbands when his income actually goes to pay for her needs and those of her children.[21] . . . When it comes to money and marriage, less may be more.[22]
>
> **Willard F. Harley, PhD**

First, the woman herself needs to choose whether she will combine her homemaking with a career. When that choice is made for her by her husband, society, or anyone else, it is likely to cause significant marital strain, and she may be deprived of the satisfaction and joy of being who she has been created to be.

Second, when a woman wants a career, she and her husband may wish to consider together whether or not to use the money she earns for basic living expenses. Considering his brain and her brain, this makes sense. A woman usually needs and wants her husband to earn the money for their basic necessities, and he is designed to do this. Dr. Willard Harley writes, "Most wives do not only expect their husbands to work, they also expect them to earn enough to support their families."[23] When a husband can't, or doesn't choose to, provide the basics for his family, it often leads to conflict in the marriage.

Simply put, a husband's failure to provide sufficient income for housing, clothing, food, transportation, and the other basics of life has the potential, given the design of his brain and her brain, to cause marital distress.

However, there are always exceptions to our suggestions. For example, while Walt furthered his education by attending medical school, I was the main breadwinner for the family. We both understood that this was a sacrifice and a short-term investment we were making together in his calling and our future. And we sensed that the Lord was pleased with our decision.

When a married couple faces the situation in which the wife has a professional career with a salary that allows her to provide the majority of the family income (and some or all of the basic family needs), the couple needs to recognize what they really face. We recommend the couple pray about it and discuss with a professional or pastoral counselor the potential risks, benefits, and consequences to their marriage and their relationship.

Third, when a couple has a child, it's time to reevaluate. This is because no matter how much we women may love our work and our career, the brain chemistry and biology of most of us will lead us to yearn to stay at home after we've had a child. As soon as my first pregnancy test came back positive, I began a debate with myself about whether to temporarily leave my career as an educator and begin my career as a homemaker and mother. I loved teaching, but I was beginning to feel my inner call to be a full-time mom. And children are designed to benefit from a mother's unique nurturing and love. Children seek and desire their mother's love, and for the vast majority of children, no one can nurture them better than their own mother.

Barb was not alone. Although 71 percent of moms work outside the home, the Pew Research Center has found that increasingly women are concerned that this may be harmful to young children. In fact, only 29 percent of women think that when both parents work full time, they can do a good job of raising a child.[24] Surprisingly, "college graduates are more negative about the increase in mothers working outside the home than those with no college experience (47 percent versus 38 percent say it is a bad thing)."[25]

Dr. Janice Shaw Crouse says, "Clearly something has to give and a family has to work together to make dual careers possible.... Far too many couples have realized—too late—that they made that choice by not having the right priorities when making important decisions. Wise women recognize that they can't have it all at once; they have to acknowledge that if they are blessed with children, it is important to give their needs top priority."[26]

> *If* you bungle raising your children, I don't think whatever else you do matters very much.[27]
>
> **Jackie Kennedy**

Researchers have shown what virtually every mom of a young child knows: for moms with kids under eighteen, their relationship to their children is the most important aspect of their lives—and it's especially true for mothers of preschool children. In fact, 80 percent of these moms say their parenting role takes precedence over all the others.[28] In her book *7 Myths of Working Mothers*, Suzanne Venker contends, "If motherhood were viewed as the full-time job it is, it would not be considered something we could do on the side, and women would be less inclined to try to balance career and motherhood, only to discover, many stress-filled years later, that it cannot be done."[29]

In my case, it was relatively easy to consider returning to the workforce after Kate's birth—at least until she was born. Once I held her, caressed her, and nursed her, I felt the overwhelming drive that women have to care for their children. I knew there was no one I could hire who would be a better caretaker for my child than me. Without the benefit of my female hormones at work in his brain, however, Walt naturally took a different approach.

The pragmatic male brain is going to question whether it makes financial sense for the mom to stay home and raise their young children. I certainly did! I bought into the argument that shouted, "The costs of raising and supporting a family are so high that to survive financially both parents *must* work." I didn't hear (or chose to ignore) those who contend, "The costs of having both parents work [real financial costs, not to mention the emotional and stress-related costs] are so high that it's usually better for the mom, the child, and the family for her to stay home."[30] Nor did I realize what the research has now clearly shown: mothers who work full time are especially burdened by time pressures and efforts to balance motherhood with other aspects of their lives.[31]

What happens to women who have to work outside the home, and on top of that, care for their husbands, their children, and their homes? Often "the result is angry, exhausted mothers desperate for a house that looks and feels like a home and for more time with their children.... Being constantly on the go in a competitive world may work for men but not for many women who want to get pregnant or who want to nurse.... Loving *is* doing something.... Who can better provide the lubricating love and nurturing than the mother?"[32]

Steven E. Rhoads, PhD

Dr. Willard Harley writes, "Some well-intentioned people, in the guise of advocating women's rights, encourage all women to develop a career, because they see employment as a right and a privilege. However, they fail to consider that a woman also has a right and privilege to be a homemaker and full-time mother."[33]

Increasing Her Emotional Security

I've come to realize that men and women both desire security — but we each need different types of security. For women, the need for security is a primary need that is hardwired into their brain circuits and hormonal responses. But their need for security isn't just about money.

Being provided for financially is important to women — so much so that many women seek part- or full-time employment to add to their husband's provision. But this need pales in comparison to the deeper need to know that their husband truly loves and cares for them and their children. When a husband provides that type of security, a woman's biology and biochemicals respond in an amazing and highly healthy fashion.

Most husbands don't understand this truth. They interpret their wife's need for security as meaning they need to work more hours and provide more things to give their families more financial security. But that is how husbands think, not how their wives think. I was surprised to find out that one study revealed that 70 percent of married women would choose to endure financial difficulties rather than to endure relational difficulties with their husband.[34]

When I thought of security as a young wife and mother, my primary thought was not about my home or checking account and our children's education. For me and most women, emotional security and relational security are what matters most to us; they are essential to our health and psyche. We are built to respond in wonderful ways when we feel emotionally safe and relationally connected to our husband. We need to know that he will be there for us no matter what.

Over the years, Barb and I have found that I can make her feel more secure and safe not only by what I do to provide for her and protect her but by what I say and the way I say it. It has taken me years, but I have learned to take to heart the wise advice of marriage and family therapist Dr. Willard Harley: "A sense of security is the bright golden thread woven through all of a woman's five basic needs. If a husband does not keep up honest and open communication with his wife, he undermines her trust and eventually destroys her security. To feel secure, a wife must trust her husband to give her accurate information about his past, the present, and the future."[35]

I've learned that when I tell Barb the truth, the whole truth, and nothing but the truth, I actually build her emotional security. Yet I've found that many husbands don't follow this tactic. They choose to "protect" their wives from the truth of their lives or from what they are feeling.

Because I know that Walt is always being truthful with me—whether talking about our finances, his concerns, how I look, or what I'm wearing—he's communicating to me that he knows I can handle the truth. Because he is truthful with me, I don't have to worry about false impressions or little white lies.

And, guys, the good news is that helping the woman in our life feel emotionally secure is much easier on us than just busting our tails to bring home more bacon. Barb and I learned this principle when Kate turned six years old.

We were just finishing dinner when my dad called to wish Kate a happy birthday. After he talked to Kate, I talked to him. When I picked up the phone, Dad simply said, "Congratulations!" For a moment I was confused. Congratulations for what? I couldn't think of a thing I had done that deserved my dad's congratulations. Then my father said something that shocked me to my core: "One-third of your life with Kate is over."

It took me a second, and then the truth of what he was communicating began to sink in. At eighteen years of age, Kate probably would leave our home. Six years already had flown by, so our celebration marked the end of one-third of her life at home. I instantly knew what my father was gently and wisely trying to communicate to me: "Son, you need to be home—to be there for your family."

I was working hard as a family physician with a busy practice—almost the equivalent of two full-time jobs. I wanted to provide for Barb and the children. I wanted to give us the best I could—a college fund, exciting vacations, a nice home and furniture. I was on my way to doing this, but I also was gone a lot.

To make a long story short, the Lord really used my dad's words to convict me of my family's need to have me at home more. I could work harder to buy more things, or I could work less but have more of me to give to them. Barb and I had long talks about the difference in what we needed and wanted, and what we thought our kids needed and wanted. I realized that being home was my *real* job.

My emotional and relational health and security were bolstered when Walt was home. Kate, Scott, and I needed Walt more than we needed the extra money he was earning. I think it was a great relief for Walt to realize that although I enjoyed the extra money, what I really needed was more of him as my best friend, husband, and father of our children.

Increasing His Emotional Security

A man's brain is hardwired and programmed for the responsibility of breadwinning and providing for his wife. The Bible calls him to this role, and his biology compels him to follow through. When he does this, he feels a great deal of satisfaction. But a man has another need that relates to his emotional security—a need for peace and quiet and domestic support on the home front.

A woman's entire system is wired and programmed for relationships, networking, talking, and sharing. So it is difficult for most women to realize how men are programmed—hardwired, if you prefer—to need space and times of peace and quiet. Although men understand that their commitment to marriage means less time for hobbies, women can contribute to their well-being by giving them at least some free time—some downtime to relax and to pursue hobbies away from home.[36] They also benefit when women make it a priority to provide an orderly and inviting home environment.

Dr. Harley writes, "The need for domestic support is a time bomb. At first, it seems irrelevant, a throwback to more primitive times."[37] Yet, in most marriages there exists an unspoken trade-off between husband and wife. Each expects the other to pitch in with domestic support. However, if he is the primary breadwinner for the home, he expects and needs his wife to attend to and care for the home and children. To the extent that she gives him this kind of domestic support, he tends to enjoy and achieve great satisfaction from his responsibility to provide his family with the income it needs.

We don't think it is old-fashioned or chauvinistic to observe that men, more often than women, have this emotional need to be cared for. And more often than not, women have the emotional need to provide such care. The male need for his wife to manage not only the care of their home and children but also his care is prevalent, persistent, and profound. Harley observes, "Traditionally, wives have assumed most household and child care responsibilities, while husbands have taken the responsibility of providing income for the family."[38] In our view, this reflects the way his brain and her brain are designed. In fact, research has shown that even in dual-career marriages, men on average do less than half as much child care and housework as their working wives.[39] Furthermore, men divorce women who are not good homemakers.[40]

Nevertheless, it is becoming important, particularly in dual-career homes, for both the husband and wife to share domestic duties as much as possible. In fact, one recent national survey reported, "Some 62 percent of adults say sharing household chores is very important to marital success. On this question, there's virtually no difference of opinion between men and women, or between older adults and younger adults."[41]

The good news is that a woman can be a powerful influence in building her man and her marriage by understanding his hormones and hardwiring when it comes to work, adventure, and domestic provision. The fact is that women are hardwired and programmed for caring for husband, family, and home. Women are built to nurture in the domestic realm.[42]

To the extent that this matches the inborn, innate design of his brain and her brain, it's good, not bad. A woman who supports and cares for her husband's emotional and domestic needs is likely to have a mate who gladly and gallantly provides for her financial and emotional security. By balancing the needs of his brain and her brain, their marriage becomes happier and stronger.

11
Chapter

His Brain — Respect;
Her Brain — Love

WHETHER HE'S SEVEN OR SEVENTY-SEVEN, A MALE'S HIGH LEVELS OF testosterone and vasopressin naturally lead him to respond to respect and admiration, appreciation and approval. When a wife understands his need for admiration and affirmation and takes note of her husband's work, hobbies, or interests, she plays a crucial role in bolstering his need to know that he is needed. No matter how great "her own achievements, it is vital to allow the man to shine, or she may not receive all the love from him she desires."[1]

A man's hardwiring and hormones lead him to sing, "Look at me! Look at what I can do," and hidden with that: "You still need me, don't you?" Working twelve hours a day, he needs to be needed.[2]

Michael Gurian

If his need to feel respected, valued, and needed by his wife is not met, a man will often abandon his wife — either physically or emotionally. If she chooses to constantly disrespect, devalue, dishonor, or disgrace him, especially in public, he will often distance himself from her. He may spend more time at work, more time with hobbies or television, more time on the computer, or

173

more time with someone—anyone—who will provide for this hormonal and hardwired need. If the disrespect and lack of admiration continue, he will eventually leave her.

I know that Walt, like all men, has a deep-seated need to be trusted and admired by his colleagues and especially by me. He will be attracted to and more deeply bonded to me as I appreciate and admire what he does for me and our children. Dr. Willard Harley reminds women that "honest admiration is a great motivator for most men. When a woman tells a man she thinks he's wonderful, that inspires him to achieve more."[3] So it is essential that I communicate to Walt, "I love when you tell and show me that you love me, but I also love the fact that you are a good husband, a good father, and so good at your work." And I like to remind women that we need to start by appreciating what our husbands are already doing well, not what they could or even should become. This is not a technique or a how-to; it is simply understanding his design.

She's Hardwired to Be Loved, Loved, Loved

Whether she's seven or seventy-seven, girls and women have brains that are designed to respond to and provide love and nurture. No relationship has a greater hormonal impact on a woman than that of being loved by a man who is committed to her for life. A man who understands this and tells his woman that he loves her plays a pivotal role in bolstering her sense that she is truly needed and loved. No matter what his own achievements, they will pale in comparison to loving his wife and children.

It is vital for a man to unreservedly and continually love his wife, to make frequent deposits into her emotional savings account. The more he deposits into this account, the more she will have available to return to him. We guys need to understand and remember that her need for repeated, recurrent, and repetitive love is simply based on her design. When she is held, hugged, and heard by her husband, she will experience a tsunami of hormones, especially oxytocin, which will increase her bonding with and desire for him. Her hardwiring and hormones lead her to say, "Hold me," "Hug me," and "Tell me you love me."

It Takes Two to Tango

The hormonal influence and hardwiring of each spouse is designed to complement and strengthen the other. As a man loves his wife and shows her affection, she is more able and willing to respect and admire him, which he's designed to respond to by loving her all the more. Marriage counselor and pastor Dr. Emerson Eggerichs describes how this works: "When a husband feels disrespected, he has a natural tendency to react in ways that feel unloving to his wife. When a wife feels unloved, she has a natural tendency to react in ways that feel disrespectful to her husband. Without love, she reacts without respect. Without respect, he reacts without love — ad nauseam."[4]

When there is conflict in a marriage, women are good at slinging verbal arrows and men are good at stonewalling. Whenever I hear myself complaining, criticizing, or crying, I am usually trying to let Walt know, "I need your love!" And whenever he gets real quiet or withdrawn or reacts harshly, he is telling me, "I need your respect!" More times than not, when Walt becomes angry at something I've said or done and I don't completely understand the cause, there's a good chance he's feeling disrespected. In a national survey, more than 80 percent of men said that when they were in a conflict with their wives, they were likely to be feeling disrespected.[5]

A man needs a wife who is a better cheerleader than she is a critic. He already gets more than enough criticism in the world. That's why behind most successful men are admiring and affirming wives. A wife needs to admire and appreciate her man for who he already is and for the positive traits he already possesses—not for who he could become or for the traits his wife wished he possessed.

Shaunti Feldhahn reminds women, "We hold incredible power—and responsibility—in our hands. We have the ability to either build up or tear down our men. We can either strengthen or hobble them in ways that go far beyond our relationship, because respect at home affects every area of a man's life.... Just as we love to hear 'I love you,' a man's heart is powerfully touched by a few simple words, 'I'm so proud of you.' "[6] King Solomon wrote, "A wife of noble character is her husband's crown, but a disgraceful wife is like decay in his bones."[7]

On the other side of the his brain/her brain coin is the fact that behind every happily married woman is a man who loves her, cherishes her, and shows gentle affection for her. The Bible teaches, "Husbands, love your wives and do not be harsh with them."[8] It's been helpful for me to understand that Barb finds my affection essential. She is designed to need and respond to gentle, affectionate words and touches from me—at least several times a day. Affection has meaning to a woman far beyond anything the average man can imagine. Barb loves the feeling she gets from her oxytocin rush when I'm affectionate toward her. This has nothing to do with sex; it has everything to do with the way she has been created.

> *To* most women, affection symbolizes security, protection, comfort, and approval, vitally important commodities in their eyes.... Affection is the environment of the marriage, while sex is an *event*. Affection is a way of life, a canopy that covers and protects a marriage.... Most women I've counseled crave affection. I try to help their husbands understand the pleasure women feel when this need is met....A woman's need for affection is probably her deepest emotional need.[9]
>
> **Willard F. Harley, PhD**

As I let Walt know how much I need him and how much I admire and respect him for what he provides for me and our family, he is better able and willing to give me the affection and intimacy to which I'm designed to respond. Our brains are designed in such a way that when we devote ourselves to the needs of our spouse, he or she is drawn to meet our needs. We are most likely to receive what we need from our spouse by providing for his or her needs.

Love is fostered and will proceed to flow out of a marriage that displays these attributes:

Do nothing out of selfish ambition or vain conceit, but in humility consider others better than yourselves. Each of you should look not only to your own interests, but also to the interests of the others.

Your attitude should be the same as that of Christ Jesus:

Who, being in very nature God,
did not consider equality with God something
to be grasped,
but made himself nothing,
taking the very nature of a servant.[10]

Both Barb and I are instructed to put aside our own selfish desires by first serving our Creator and then by serving each other and providing for each other's needs. If we choose not to follow this course, our marriage begins to weaken.

The Bible gives a reason why we are seeing so many disordered marriages, even in our faith communities: "For where you have envy and selfish ambition, there you find disorder and every evil practice."[11] If you seek to meet your own needs or demand that your spouse meet your needs without our first seeking to meet his or her needs, it will likely lead to disorder or the eventual destruction of your marriage. Our Creator, who designed the brains, roles, needs, strengths, weaknesses, and blind spots of each sex, presents a different plan in the Bible: in marriage, the husband and the wife should "be subject to one another."[12]

He's Responsible for Sacrificial Love

The Bible tells husbands to "love your wives, just as Christ loved the church and gave himself up for her."[13] In other words, I am to love Barb in the same way God loves me. I am to give myself in sacrificial love to Barb, as Christ sacrificed himself for me. The Bible also says, "Husbands ought to love their wives as their own bodies. He who loves his wife loves himself. After all, no one ever hated his own body, but he feeds and cares for it, just as Christ does the church—for we are members of his body."[14] So I am to love my wife as my own body—for indeed she is one with me. Finally, the Bible teaches, "Husbands, love your wives and do not be harsh with them."[15]

"Job One" for a husband is to sacrificially love his wife—above his work, children, recreation, or hobbies. After our personal relationship with God, our wife is Priority One. Is this easy? Nope. At times it can seem impossible (at least it is in our *own* power and strength). This is not just a man-sized job; it's a God-sized job. It requires God's supernatural love acting in and through us.

I've practiced loving Barb through the years by using some of what are known as the "one another" (or "each other") verses in Scripture (there are over forty of them). When I substitute the word "Barb" for the words "one another," these verses paint a very high standard for me in sacrificially loving her. I don't always get it right, but table 5 shows just a few of the ways I've chosen to demonstrate my love for Barb.

Table 5 — "One Another" Verses

Scriptural Encouragement	What I'm Working On
Be at peace with Barb.[16]	I'm learning how to communicate with her and how to disagree with her agreeably.
Be devoted to Barb.[17]	I touch base with her during my workday and avoid situations in which I would be alone with another woman.
Encourage Barb.[18]	I find a variety of ways to communicate my love to her every day — whether with words or a hug.
Build Barb up.[19]	I find ways to praise her every day for all she does for me and our children.
Serve Barb humbly in love.[20]	I communicate my love to her by finding small ways to serve her each day, such as getting up early to make her coffee every morning.
Honor Barb above myself.[21]	I speak highly of her to others and am learning to be better in avoiding put-downs or teasing in public.
Greet Barb with a holy kiss.[22]	I kiss her when I wake up, when I leave the house, when I arrive home, and at bedtime.
Seek to never provoke Barb.[23]	I keep an eye out for things that bother Barb and try to avoid them whenever possible.
Forgive Barb.[24]	I'm learning how to both forgive and forget. When I get angry or irritated with Barb, I work to not bring up old grievances, to not "get historical."
Be patient with Barb.[25]	I've had to adjust expectations and make them more realistic. I love her by waiting for her.
Bear with Barb.[26]	I work to not *be* a bear with her.

To the female brain, love is nourishment. It's her sustenance. She cannot bloom without it. She cannot shine if you don't provide it.

She's Responsible for Sacrificial Respect

The Creator of the male brain makes our key role as wives absolutely clear when he instructs, "The wife must respect her husband."[27] While Walt is directed to sacrificially love me, I am to respect Walt sacrificially. According to the divine design, respecting her husband is a wife's "Job One." This may seem impossible at times! Yet he cannot thrive without it.

> *The* male need for respect and admiration—especially from his woman—is so hardwired and so critical that most men would rather feel unloved than disrespected or inadequate.[28]
>
> **Shaunti Feldhahn**

A man is designed to respond positively to his wife's sacrificial respect and admiration in the same way we are designed to respond to him when he loves, honors, nourishes, and cherishes us. Part of the divine design for holy, joyful, and contented marriages is for wives, as a demonstration of our sacrificial respect for our husbands, to encourage and enable them to provide leadership in our marriage. However, this is not a woman-sized job; it's a God-sized job. It requires God's supernatural love working in and through us.

I've had the opportunity to meet hundreds of women who are strong, capable, and extremely talented. But a woman who tries to prove these traits by dominating her husband will actually drive him away. If a woman chooses to lead, govern, or rule in her marriage, she ought not to be surprised if she knocks him out of the marriage.

Jessica is a close friend of mine. She's a strong, attractive, and extremely talented woman. She is well educated and has two beautiful children. Anything a man could do at her workplace, she, quite frankly, could do better. After all, that's how she was raised—to be strong, to earn her way, to obtain respect. Unfortunately for her husband, she failed to realize how much she and her children were designed to need him to lead them at home. Through her nagging, constant disrespect and ridicule, he was beaten down to an ineffective, disengaged sorry shadow of the husband he could have been to her.

To keep respect for Walt a priority in my marriage:

- *I've chosen to follow, to the best of my ability and with God's help, God's divine design for me and my marriage.*
- *I've chosen to demonstrate my feminine strength and talent by respecting Walt and encouraging and enabling him to lead me and our children.*
- *I've chosen to follow him—and to do everything in my power to let him be the leader in our family he was designed to be.*
- *When tempted to be the leader of our family, I've chosen instead to pray for Walt, myself, and our marriage.*
- *I've chosen to speak well of him when I am with him and to speak only positively of him when I am with my female friends.*
- *I've chosen to be strong in my support of him.*
- *I've chosen to cheer him on rather than criticize and critique him.*

I believe these choices make our marriage much stronger and more satisfying.

Love Is Greek to Me

The Bible condenses everything we're saying in this chapter into a single verse: "Each one of you also must love his wife as he loves himself, and the wife must respect her husband."[29] When Paul instructs husbands to "love" their wives, he is using the Greek verb *agapaō*. This verb is used in this verse in an ongoing sense. It could be translated, "go on loving," "continuously love," or "keep on loving." The Creator recognizes the need he created in the brain and heart of every woman and that this need continues throughout her life.

The Greek word translated "respect" is *phobeomai*, which means to "be in awe of" or "revere." Not only are women to highly regard their husband; they also must highly value them.

"All You Need Is Love"

Greek writers used several different words to convey aspects of "love."

- *Storgē* describes affection, especially between family members — such as a parent's love for a child.
- *Philandros* describes the affection of a wife for a husband.
- *Philoteknos* describes the affection of a mother for her children.
- *Eros* describes romantic, passionate love (but can also mean erotic or sexual love) — such as the desiring love between husband and wife.
- *Phileō* describes deep friendship, loyalty, or affection for family or dear friends.
- *Agapē* (or the verb form, *agapaō*) is the type of love God gives to us and the love a husband is to give to and for his wife. It means to love in a sacrificial or moral sense.

Theologian Avery Cardinal Dulles writes, "*Eros* and *agapē* belong together as two phases of ideal love. If we did not receive, we would have nothing to give; and if we were not disposed to give, we would be spiritually unprepared to receive. In their highest expression, the two types of love reinforce each other."[30]

God knows the needs of your husband's brain and that your husband is designed to respond to your respect and admiration, especially when it is shown through your actions and words. I believe this respect is to be as sacrificial as the love God instructs our husbands to lavish on us.

Why is there no teaching in the Bible for a wife to agapaō *her husband? I think it's because the Lord has created a woman to sacrificially love and nurture — after all, we are wired this way. Sensitivity and compassion are all part of her brain's designed nature. The Creator does not have to instruct her to do what he created her to do in the first place.*

However, the Bible does instruct older women to "encourage the young women to love [philandros] their husbands, to love [philoteknos] their children."[31]

How to Love and Respect Each Other

When it comes to respect and admiration, men consistently describe three key needs:

1. Respect my judgment.
2. Respect my ability.
3. Respect me in public.[32]

The next time your husband stubbornly drives in circles, ask yourself what is more important: being on time to the party or his feeling trusted. No contest.[33]

Shaunti Feldhahn

When it comes to love, women consistently describe five key needs:

1. Tell me you love me by continually paying attention to me.
2. Tell me you love me by continually pursuing me.
3. Tell me you love me by continually holding and hugging me.
4. Tell me you love me by continually helping me around the house and with the children.
5. Tell me you love me by telling me I'm beautiful to you.[34]

A woman becomes beautiful when she knows she's loved.... Cut off from love, rejected, no one pursuing her, something in a woman wilts like a flower no one waters anymore.[35]

Stasi Eldredge

Divinely Designed to Complement Each Other

Now just to be clear, wives need the respect and admiration of their husbands. In fact, the Bible teaches, "Husbands,... treat [your wives] with respect."[36]

And men need lots of love and affection from their wives. In fact, the Bible instructs women "to love [*philandros*] their husbands."[37] But the basic and primary need of the male brain is to receive and respond to her respect and admiration.

And the basic and primary need of the female brain is to receive and respond to his (*agapē*) love.

A wife's brain and hormones are designed to respond to her husband's love. My job as a loving husband is to be my wife's mirror—to reflect to her how lovely she is to me and to her Creator. I know she longs to hear these things not only in words but in romantic gestures as well—flowers, cards, calls, dates, dinners, time together, help with chores, and conversation.

My husband's brain is created to respond when I say, "I admire and respect you. I trust you to lead our family. I appreciate all you do for me and the children. Thank you for your hard work. Thank you for loving me well." He not only needs to hear me tell him these things, but he responds dramatically when he hears me telling others these things about him.

He feels great pleasure when he is respected and admired. When he knows I respect and admire him and appreciate that he knows my needs and expectations, he usually bends over backward to make me happy. And the more he loves me, the more I'm able to love him.

Conversely, the more I fully understand Walt's design and creation, the easier it is for me to understand him and to make him happy. And when he senses my respect, trust, and admiration, he is fully able to sense my deepest love for him. Then he wants to love me better, and I want to love him more. Our love for each other is designed to grow deeper, wider, and more wonderful.

PART 4

His Brain,

The Beauty
of God's Design

12

Chapter

Created to Be One
by God's Design

THE MORE WE LEARN ABOUT THE SCIENCE OF HOW THE BRAIN WORKS, the more we are amazed by what a wonderful gift God has given us to enjoy in his design for marriage. Now that we've shared some of how his brain and her brain function, let's turn to the creation story and explore in a bit more depth what the Bible reveals about the Creator's hand in designing his brain and her brain.

The Bible tells us how the first man, Adam, was created: "The LORD God formed the man from the dust of the ground and breathed into his nostrils the breath of life, and the man became a living being."[1] The Hebrew word translated "formed" is *yatsar*, which literally means to "squeeze into shape" or "mold into a form." It is most commonly used to describe what happens when a potter forms a clay pot or an earthen jar. Hebrew scholars say it can also be translated as to "determine" or "fashion, form, frame, make, or purpose."[2]

The Bible uses a completely different term to describe the creation of the first woman: "Then the LORD God made a woman."[3] Moses tells us that God did not create woman in the same way he created man. God did not *yatsar* or "form" woman like he did man; he *banah*-ed her. This Hebrew word, which is usually translated "made," "built," or "fashioned,"[4] describes a completely different design.

Banah means, literally and figuratively, to "complexly design and build." In other Scripture references, it is used to describe the intricate construction of the temple, an altar, a home, or a city. It is used to describe the planned design and building of complex, beautiful necessities. The craftsmen *banah*-ed Solomon's temple, for example.

Unlike man, who was squeezed or formed by the Creator's hand, the woman was designed and crafted differently. Man was *molded* out of the clay, but the woman's creation is compared to the creation, design, and workmanship of architectural arts and masterpieces.

This difference in the creation of woman helps me understand why Scripture describes the husband as the wife's protector. She is a very delicate and valuable work of art. He is the package designed to envelop and guard her—to preserve her from scrapes and nicks, from cuts and abuses that would detract from her beauty and value.

Like clay, man is molded; like precious artwork, woman is designed and built for beauty, stability, and durability. He is rural and practical; she is the jewel, the crown. Science *and* Scripture both seem to indicate that from conception onward, male and female—his brain and her brain—are distinctly different.

She Is Adam's Counterpart

Moses tells us that at the end of each day of creation prior to creating man, "God saw that it was good."[5] But after God placed man in the garden of Eden, man was alone. The Creator saw this, and, Moses records, "The Lord God said, 'It is not good for the man to be alone. I will make a helper suitable for him.' "[6]

One scholar notes that "when God concluded that he would create another creature so that man would not be alone, he decided to make 'a power equal to him,' someone whose [emotional, relational, and spiritual] strength was equal to man's. Woman was not intended to be merely man's helper. She was to be instead his partner."⁷

The two Hebrew words that make up the phrase translated "helper suitable" can also mean "an equal or perfect match," "an exquisitely dovetailed opposite," or "a helper who is just right for him." Sometimes you will hear people use the term *helpmeet* or *helpmate* as if they are compound words. However, in the original language they are two separate words that convey a somewhat different meaning.

The noun translated "helper" in most modern translations is the Hebrew word *ezer*. It can mean "one who succors." The word *succor*, an old-fashioned term, connotes the idea of "one who saves from extremity," "one who delivers from death," "help or relief rendered in danger," or "one who affords relief."

This word can describe the action of someone who gives water to a person dying of thirst. It describes one who places a tourniquet on the arm of a bleeding person, thereby saving his or her life. The word evokes an entirely different notion from the idea of an employee or domestic help. Because the English word *helper* can connote so many different ideas, it can fail to convey accurately the true meaning of the Hebrew word *ezer*. The Hebrew term does not suggest the subordinate role that the English word *helper* can suggest.

Far from being a subordinate or menial servant, the woman is actually described as the rescuer of man—one who releases him from the bondage of aloneness, from the inefficiency and ineffectiveness of living and ministering alone. This truly is an amazing pronouncement. Why? Apart from this passage, the word *ezer* is used in the Bible to describe only the work of God himself! God is the succor, the *ezer* or helper, of Israel in the time of distress. He is the "helper," the *ezer*, who does for his people what we cannot do for ourselves—the one who meets our needs.

One commentary points out, "In this context the word seems to express the idea of an 'indispensable companion.' The woman would supply what the man was lacking in the design of creation, and logically it would follow that the man would supply what she was lacking, although that is not stated here."[8] We are not to infer from this that the Creator made a mistake—far from it! Rather, he created in the male and female a designed need for his or her other. She is our Father's perfectly designed and created gift to man—our perfect match.

The woman as man's helper, as revealed in the original language used by Moses, is the wife who brings completeness to her husband. It is she who is designed and created to bring him "salvation" from his aloneness, protection from his blind spots, and strength in areas in which he is weak.

> Many Hebrews, both ancient and modern, consider aloneness as the negation of authentic living. To them, true life is not individual, but corporate and social.... The Hebrew word translated as "alone" ["it is not good for the man to be alone"] carries an overtone of separation and even alienation.... The Hebrew mind-set was that human beings live only insofar as they are related within their environment to people with whom they share life and love.[9]
>
> **Samuel Terrien**

We also need to pay attention to the word translated "suitable," the Hebrew word *neged*. *Neged* can literally be translated "for what is in front of him" or more specifically "an opposite part; specifically a counterpart, or mate." *Neged* (or *k^e neged o*) literally means "according to the opposite of him." Translations that use words such as "suitable" or "suitable for," "matching," or "corresponding to" all seem to capture the idea.

The picture here is that a woman is not created to be behind her man or even beside him. Rather, she is pictured as being in front of and facing him. She and he are perfectly matched. She is a superlatively dovetailed ally, accomplice, and comrade. But as is so consistent with his character, God does not force her on Adam. After all, he created the male and knows that he will need to figure this out on his own. So the Lord God lovingly waits until Adam realizes just how needy he is: "So the man gave names to all the livestock, the birds of the air and all the beasts of the field. But for Adam no suitable helper was found."[10]

In all of creation, Adam did not find his *ezer neged*. So "God caused the man to fall into a deep sleep; and while he was sleeping, he took one of the man's ribs and closed up the place with flesh. Then the LORD God made a woman from the rib he had taken out of the man, and he brought her to the man."[11]

This divine report of creation, with its beautiful and carefully constructed poetic language, shows the creation of woman as a being built to match her man. She is attuned to him and is gifted so that her strengths match his weaknesses and her vision matches his blind spots. No wonder the Creator stated, when he looked at man, "It is not good for the man to be alone."[12]

The story not only portrays her as delivering him from the void of alienation and aloneness, it subtly describes the whole of a potential relationship between one man and one woman that can only be contained within a lifelong sacrificial relationship—what Scripture will later call marriage.

My Oh My Oh My!

God created and gave to Adam exactly what he needed even before Adam fully realized his need. After creating her, "the LORD God ... brought her to the man."[13]

Adam, seeing for the first time the curves and beauty of the naked woman, is caught slack-jawed. He is flabbergasted. He gasps. The Larimore paraphrase of Adam's words goes like this:

Wow! My oh my oh my! Right in the nick of time! This feminine, sexy work of art is awesome! This special one is my other,
to be part of me, to complete me—strong where I am weak,
weak where I am strong. My match! My perfect match!

The usual translations, however, are a bit drier: "The man
said, 'This is now bone of my bones and flesh of my flesh.' "[14]

The expressions "bone of my bones" and "flesh of my flesh"
refer not to the woman as a secondary creature taken from the
primary one but to a total and complete relationship. "Bone" and
"flesh" communicate a spectrum of human characteristics from
the strength of bone to the softness of flesh—a complex mixture
of both power and weakness, some strong attributes and some
weaker ones, within each sex.

As you can imagine, bones without flesh (tendons, nerves, and
muscle) are as useless as flesh without bones. The design of bones
and flesh, husband and wife, is that they are stronger and more
effective together than apart. The divine design is that a man and
woman in marriage, working together, are equal but complementary parts of a potentially strong and amazing whole.

Adam Becomes a Husband

Adam goes on to exclaim, "She shall be called 'woman,' for she
was taken out of man."[15] The language Adam uses takes a dramatic change that is completely missed in English. Up to this
moment in the creation story, the "man" or "human being" (in
Hebrew, *adam*), who had been alone and incomplete, now is described as what I call "a true man."

In the Hebrew, Adam is now called *iysh* (pronounced "eesh")
—a word that describes the man with very particular roles. He
now accepts the role of husband, mate, partner, protector, and
provider for what was designed to be his most valuable and honored belonging—his woman—now called in Hebrew *ishah*.

Moses tells us in a very clever way how men and women are to be both delightfully and complementarily different while at the same time one. This can happen only in marriage—a divinely instituted, one-man-one-woman relationship of purpose, exchange, and sharing. Woman was created to rescue man from his aloneness and incompleteness. She was also carefully designed to respond to him and to create a response in him.

That's why we believe God made woman in a completely different way than he made man. He designed man and woman delightfully different and differently so that they might complete, match, and strengthen each other. Without woman, man was not, is not, and will not be all he can be.

This ancient biblical narrative is literally as fresh as today's science. It points to both the ideal monogamy and the ideal of monogamy —of a man and woman joined together as one flesh—as husband and wife.

Leave and Cleave

Moses continued his creation narrative by making what would have been a stunning pronouncement to the people of his day: "For this reason a man will leave his father and mother and be united to his wife, and they will become one flesh."[16]

In the ancient Near Eastern cultures, to honor one's father and mother was a most sacred obligation. In dramatic contrast, the Creator's unambiguous command is that a man who is married owes his first loyalty to his wife.

Furthermore, the language of Moses makes it clear that a man is to do more than just *leave* his parents. The Hebrew word translated "leave" actually means he is to "abandon" his father and his mother in favor of his wife. His duty shifts from his parentage to his marriage, setting the stage for the completion of the thought that the man will "be united to his wife, and they will become one flesh." The message could not be clearer: a man cannot "cling" to both his parents—especially his mother—and his wife. Each boy must psychologically leave his mother to become a man. This process is stimulated by the boy's testosterone and vasopressin, but it must be encouraged and facilitated by *both* his mother and his father.

A healthy marriage has to carefully blend his brain's biological drive for independence and self-reliance with her brain's overwhelming biological drive for bonding and attachment. But achieving this balance is much more difficult if the mother-son/father-daughter separation is not complete. Barb dramatized the need for leaving and cleaving for our son, Scott, and his fiancée, Jennifer, at their rehearsal dinner.

Before Walt and I stood to make our comments and our toast to the young couple, I put on an apron and explained to Scott, Jennifer, and our guests that I had been praying for Scott and for his wife-to-be—and for the day when he would leave me to cleave to her—since they were babies.

Turning toward Scott, I told him that I was not his confidante or go-to girl anymore; that job was now Jennifer's. I then reached into the apron pocket and pulled out a large pair of scissors and handed them to Walt. He cut the apron strings and handed them to me. I presented them to Jennifer with these words: "Jennifer, I hand you the apron strings—and I give to you my son."

As Jennifer and Barb hugged, there were few dry eyes in the house—especially mine. I don't know that I've ever been more grateful for my wife's wisdom.

"To cleave" or "to unite" designates not only the beginning of a new covenant but also the maintenance of that covenant. It means not only to "cling to," or "adhere to," but to "stick with." The Hebrew word for "one flesh" indicates that becoming one flesh is a process of physical, emotional, relational, and spiritual development that deepens in intensity and strengthens with the passage of time.

And as we strengthen our bonds with each other, we also want to strengthen our bonds with God. King Solomon made this powerful observation:

> Two are better than one,
>   because they have a good return for their work:
> If one falls down,
>   his friend can help him up.
> But pity the man who falls
>   and has no one to help him up!
> Also, if two lie down together, they will keep warm.
>   But how can one keep warm alone?
> Though one may be overpowered,
>   two can defend themselves.
> A cord of three strands is not quickly broken."[17]

We have always considered God to be the third strand of the cord of our marriage. Marriage, at its best, as designed by the Creator, is not just the melding of his brain and her brain—but his brain, her brain, *and* the Creator's brain. A cord of three strands is not easily broken.

But the cord is easily stretchable; God is the strength and stability in our marriage. Consistently trusting him to lead us and our family provides us a steadfast purpose, a firm foundation, solid direction and support, and an eternal hope. In times of conflict (yes, we have had many), we've found it critical to keep our eyes and our hope on God and his divine design for each of us and our marriage—to direct us away from our own selfish point of view and to lead us to the blessings of strength, security, and satisfaction that can only come by recognizing and following his design. We have found that the inevitable result of a man and woman growing closer to God is that they grow closer to each other.

13

Chapter

Cherish, Honor, Nurture
by God's Design

ONE OF MY FAVORITE BIBLICAL CHARACTERS IS PETER. I SHARE MANY temperament features with him, especially his blind spots and faults.

Although he is often portrayed as gruff and crass, I think Peter writes with an uncanny understanding of women.

In his first letter, Peter writes, "Husbands,... treat [your wives] with respect"[1] or, as another version says, "You husbands ..., show her honor."[2] The Greek word that is translated "honor" or "respect" means to "value," "attach high value," and "treasure." It describes an action that involves a husband esteeming his wife to the highest degree—as someone who is precious or priceless.

This is not a word that describes an emotion; it's a word that connotes an action. We will develop strong feelings for whatever we treasure. Psychological studies show that when a person makes a decision to honor and value something, his or her feelings will start changing within six weeks. In other words, something happens emotionally to a man as he continually values and treasures his wife. The very act of valuing and treasuring alters his emotions.

> *W*here your pleasure is, there is your treasure: where your treasure, there your heart; where your heart, there your happiness.[3]
>
> **Augustine**

Mysteriously, and at the same time, something powerful happens to a woman when a man values and treasures her. I believe this is why Peter commands men to treasure their wives.

Woman, a Very Special Vessel

But that's not all Peter says. "Husbands,... be considerate as you live with your wives, and treat them with respect as the weaker partner."[4] The Greek word usually translated "weaker" is said by experts in Greek to be somewhat difficult to render in English. Literally, the Greek word *asthenēs* can describe someone who is without strength, feeble, sickly, or unwell—someone who is diseased, impotent, or weak.[5]

Although Barb and I are not theologians, we both felt in our hearts that a man like Peter, at least as we see him, would not ask men to honor or value weakness. In addition, this was a real conundrum to me. How could I honor and value something feeble? It just didn't make sense to me.

One day I was in the physicians' lounge of our local hospital, having a cup of coffee with a psychiatrist friend named Peter, who had grown up in Greece. Peter was my local expert in the Greek language, so I asked him how he interpreted the Greek word *asthenēs*. As he explained the various descriptions of the word to me, I was pleasantly surprised to discover a much richer and deeper meaning. He said this term could be used to describe

- the most fragile and valuable art
- the most delicate and costly bone china, porcelain vases, and crystal
- the most valuable and exquisite jewelry

He went on to say that the term is used to describe a dainty, delicate, luxurious, ethereal, subtle but extremely rare and dear gift.

Men, we wouldn't say a 1957 Porsche is "weak." We would not say the *Mona Lisa* is "weak." These items would be described as *asthenēs*—priceless pieces of beautiful artistry, belongings of immense and incredible importance, worth, and value. These artworks are designed, intended, and crafted to be appreciated, beloved, and desired; to be honored, esteemed, and valued; to be appreciated, respected, and protected; to be sheltered, shielded, and praised; to be proclaimed, lifted up, and spotlighted; and to be polished, displayed, and treasured.

Wow! Peter is saying that God has built for and given to each husband a priceless and delicate treasure—his wife—for him to value, esteem, and care for. If you're married, God has given you a spouse that he intended and created for you—a woman of indescribable, inconceivable, inestimable, and incredible value. And men, the owner of the art gallery—our heavenly Father—holds us responsible for our wives' care. He holds us responsible for caring for and caring deeply about them.

Men—Nourish and Cherish Your Wife

A man's responsibilities for the treasure God has given him in his wife don't end with loving and caring for her. Paul goes on to command in the book of Ephesians, the divinely inspired words on balancing faith and family, that we husbands are not only to love (*agapaō*) our wives but to "feed and care for [them], just as Christ does the church."[6] The Greek word translated "feed" is also translated "nourish" in other versions. It gives a wonderful picture of another responsibility in honoring our wives. The Greek word is *ektrephō*, and it means to "rear up to maturity," "train," "bring up," or "nourish."

Do you want to know how to nourish your wife? Earlier we talked about the "one another" verses as a way we can use to demonstrate our love for each other. However, some of these "one another" instructions provide husbands with clues about how to nourish our wives. The wise man will look them up, study them, and practice them. At least three of these verses deal with the kind of spiritual nourishing Paul commands:

- "instruct [our wives]"[7]
- "teach [our wives]"[8]
- "speak to [our wives] with psalms, hymns and spiritual songs"[9]

It is not our pastor's role to be the primary spiritual teacher for our family. We husbands are given this awesome privilege and responsibility—to nourish not only our wives but also our children.[10] In our family, this has meant that at various times Barb and I have studied the Bible, a devotional, or an inspirational book together. I've taught small groups in our home. I use family meals as a time to discuss biblical principles. And it has meant times of both family worship at home as well as engaging in worship together as a family in church.

Walt's spiritual leadership in our home has not only allowed our family to learn and practice biblical principles but has given me the joy of seeing my children respond to their father's direction and teaching. Talk about an oxytocin rush! In addition, it has made me feel not only spiritually nourished by him but loved in a tangible way.

Paul goes on to give husbands another marital responsibility: to "cherish" their wives. The Greek word usually translated "cherish" is *thalpō*. It literally means to "brood" or "warm."[11]

City slickers may think of "brooding" as "pondering deeply or moodily." But the word is primarily an agrarian term used to describe a bird sitting on eggs to incubate them as they grow, mature, and develop. It's also used to describe the action of an adult bird as it protects its young by pulling them to its soft, warm, down-covered breast and covering them with its protective wings. In fact, in a psalm describing the security God provides, the psalmist uses a brooding image as well: "He will cover you with his feathers, and under his wings you will find refuge."[12] Brooding is a sacrificial and loving way to protect the precious chicks from the elements. It is a beautiful image of a husband's love that leads him to cherish his wife, the precious gift God has given to him.

We husbands need to take seriously the admonitions of both Peter and Paul to honor, cherish, and nurture our wives. In fact, Peter follows his teaching with a stunning warning: "Be good husbands to your wives. Honor them, delight in them. As women they lack some of your advantages. But in the new life of God's grace, you're equals. Treat your wives, then, as equals so your prayers don't run aground."[13]

Honoring, respecting, and caring for Barb is such an important commission and calling that if I, as her husband, choose not to do it, then Peter tells me that my prayers will be hindered. God apparently doesn't want me ever to forget that he blessed me with an amazing gift by giving me my wife. If I want my relationship with God to be all that he created it to be, I need to honor, value, and respect the gift he designed specifically for me.

The Marriage Box

Barb and I have learned that a husband needs to cherish, honor, and nurture his wife, and a wife needs to respect and admire her husband. This is so essential to a healthy marriage that we give friends who are getting married a beautiful but empty box. Inside it we place this nugget of wisdom that we adapted from the writings of J. Allan Petersen:[14]

Most people get married believing a myth—that marriage is a beautiful box full of all the things we have longed for: companionship, sexual fulfillment, intimacy, friendship. And that somehow the box mysteriously remains full of those goodies.

———

We believe the marriage license is the key to this box. We can take from it as much as we want, and it somehow mysteriously remains full.

———

The truth is that marriage, at the start, is an empty box. You must put something in before you can take anything out. If you do not put into the box more than you take out, it becomes empty.

———

There is no love in marriage; love is in people, and people put it into marriage.

———

Romance, consideration, generosity aren't in marriage; they are in people, and people put them into the marriage box.

———

After marriage, we start to empty the box, believing our spouse will fill it again. But it won't happen, at least not for long. The box gets empty, disappointment sets in, and the relationship takes a nosedive.

———

When the box gets empty, we become vulnerable for an affair or a divorce.

———

A couple must learn the art and form the habit of giving, loving, serving, praising—keeping the box full. If you take out more than you put in, the box will get empty.

———

Love is something you do—an activity directed toward your mate. It takes two to keep the box full.

We cannot do this alone. We need each other's help, support, urging, and encouragement. However, most of all, we need God's help. As each of us seeks to grow closer to him, we will find ourselves growing closer to each other — in a bond that none can break, with a marriage box truly filled to overflowing.

We encourage married couples to fill their "marriage box" daily with the "one anothers." Let it remind you, men, to love and nourish and cherish your wife. Let it remind you, wives, to respect and admire your husband. Let it be a reminder that your marriage can, by God's grace and your commitment, be all that God designed it to be.

A Final Reminder

Happy and satisfying marriages are those in which the husband and wife are content and comfortable and continuously working on their relationship. We believe the work of building a marriage is easier when we understand the divine design of marriage and the delightful and created differences in the male and female brain. These differences strongly attract us to each other, but, if we're not careful, they can also drive us apart.

But our differences don't have to drive us apart. I like the perspective that rock musician Van Halen expressed when asked about the differences among the members of his band: "Yeah, we have our differences, but we put those aside, and now we're making music. It's great."[15]

That's it! Men and women are different. Our prayer has been, and continues to be, that this book will help you recognize the dissimilarities, disparities, divergences, discrepancies, and distinctions between his brain and her brain — that you will understand them as Creator composed and then make great music as a married couple.

We have aimed to explore the fundamental differences between his brain and her brain in a way that will help husbands and wives understand why relationships between the two genders can be so infuriating and frustrating. As John Gray, author of *Men Are from Mars, Women Are from Venus*, has observed, "When men and women are able to respect and accept their differences, then love has a chance to blossom."[16] We would add that when husbands and wives understand the differences between their brain biology and biochemistry, they will be able to more clearly see and understand how they are designed to become one.

We hope that those who may pick up this book in order to manipulate, manage, or modify their spouses will see that they are missing the mark of God's divine plan for marriage. And we hope that those, especially women, who may fear that our plea for couples to discover and live according to our biological, divinely designed differences will see that this understanding does not doom women to "traditional" roles. Rather, our belief is that God's design of the male and female brain and his blueprint for marriage actually set us free to be exactly who God created us to be.

By ourselves, we are unlikely to succeed in having the best marriage possible. The secret of success when it comes to marital happiness and satisfaction is to accept the plan and assistance of our Creator who designed us, made us, and instituted marriage in the first place.

The Bible tells us that we are terribly flawed and selfish to our core. Our hearts are "deceitful above all things and beyond cure. Who can understand it?"[17] Yet the Bible also tells us that our Creator wants to change us and our marriages. God declares, "I will give you a new heart and put a new spirit in you; I will remove from you your heart of stone and give you a heart of flesh. And I will put my Spirit in you and move you to follow my decrees and be careful to keep my laws.... you will be my people, and I will be your God."[18]

God's divine design—the fascinating interplay of his brain and her brain loving and respecting each other and becoming one together—is the only design by which a man and a woman can come to a life and marriage that is rich and deeply satisfying. The Creator's plan is that my brain is designed to truly love, honor, nourish, and cherish Barb ...

And my brain is designed to truly respect, admire, and encourage Walt ...

So that she is fully woman ...

And he is fully man.

Sources

Introduction

1. [pg. 24] Katharine Hepburn, *Brainy Quote: www.brainyquote.com/quotes/ quotes/k/katharineh100498.html* (April 12, 2007).

Chapter 1: Different by Divine Design

1. [pg. 28] Adapted from Lynne Truss, *Eats, Shoots and Leaves: The Zero Tolerance Approach to Punctuation* (New York: Gotham Books, 2004), 9.
2. [pg. 29] America On-Line poll, conducted December 2005.
3. [pg. 29] Barbara and Allan Pease, *Why Men Don't Listen and Women Can't Read Maps: How We're Different and What to Do about It* (New York: Broadway Books, 2000), 5–6.
4. [pg. 30] Anne Moir and David Jessel, *Brain Sex: The Real Difference Between Men and Women* (New York: Dell, 1992), 5.
5. [pg. 30] Simon Baron-Cohen, *The Essential Difference: The Truth about the Male and Female Brain* (New York: Basic Books, 2003), 1.
6. [pg. 30] Quoted in Joe Garofoli, "Femme Mentale: San Francisco Neuropsychiatrist Says Differences Between Women's and Men's Brains Are Very Real, and the Sooner We All Understand It, the Better." Posted August 6, 2006: A–1. *San Francisco Chronicle: http://sfgate.com/cgi-bin/ article.cgi?file=/c/a/2006/08/06/MNG3HKAMVO1.DTL* (April 12, 2007).
7. [pg. 30] Moir and Jessel, *Brain Sex*, 20.
8. [pg. 31] Psalm 139:13–16.
9. [pg. 31] Cited in Steven E. Rhoads, *Taking Sex Differences Seriously* (San Francisco: Encounter Books, 2004), 23.
10. [pg. 32] Quoted in Ronald Kotulak, "Gender and the Brain: New Evidence Shows How Hormones Wire the Minds of Men and Women to See the World Differently," *Chicago Tribune*, April 30, 2006. View online at *http://www.rci.rutgers.edu/~shors/pdf/gender_brain_Apr30_2006.pdf* (August 1, 2007).
11. [pg. 33] R. A. Gorski, "Sexual Differentiation of the Brain," *Hospital Practice* 13, no. 10 (October 1978): 55–62.
12. [pg. 33] S. Hofer and J. Frahm, "Topography of the Human Corpus Callosum Revisited—Comprehensive Fiber Tractography Using Diffusion Tensor Magnetic Resonance Imaging," *Journal of Neuroimaging* 32, no. 3 (September 2006): 989–94.
13. [pg. 33] R. Achiron and A. Achiron, "Development of the Human Fetal Corpus Callosum: A High-Resolution, Cross-Sectional Sonographic Study," *Ultrasound in Obstetrics and Gynecology* 18, no. 4 (October 2001): 343–47.

14. [pg. 33] S. J. Hwang et al., "Gender Differences in the Corpus Callosum of Neonates," *NeuroReport* 15, no. 6 (April 29, 2004): 1029–32. See also R. Achiron, S. Lipitz, and A. Achiron, "Sex-Related Differences in the Development of the Human Fetal Corpus Callosum: In Utero Ultrasonographic Study," *Prenatal Diagnosis* 21, no. 2 (February 2001): 116–20.

15. [pg. 33] M. C. Tuncer, E. S. Hatipoglu, and M. Ozates, "Sexual Dimorphism and Handedness in the Human Corpus Callosum Based on Magnetic Resonance Imaging," *Surgical and Radiologic Anatomy* 27, no. 3 (August 2005): 254–59. See also A. Dubb et al., "Characterization of Sexual Dimorphism in the Human Corpus Callosum," *NeuroImage* 20, no. 1 (September 2003): 512–19.

16. [pg. 34] "Sex Differences Found in Proportions of Gray and White Matter in the Brain: Links to Differences in Cognitive Performance Seen." Posted May 18, 1999. *Science Daily: www.sciencedaily.com/releases/1999/05/990518072823.htm* (April 12, 2007).

17. [pg. 34] Elizabeth Heubeck, "How Male and Female Brains Differ: Researchers Reveal Sex Differences in the Brain's Form and Function." Posted April 11, 2005. *WebMD Feature: www.medicinenet.com/script/main/art.asp?articlekey=50512* (April 12, 2007).

18. [pg. 34] "Sex Differences Found in Proportions of Gray and White Matter."

19. [pg. 34] P. Dewing et al., "Sexually Dimorphic Gene Expression in Mouse Brain Precedes Gonadal Differentiation," *Molecular Brain Research* 118, no. 1–2 (October 21, 2003): 82–90.

20. [pg. 35] "Brain May 'Hard-Wire' Sexuality Before Birth." Posted October 22, 2003. *Science Daily: www.sciencedaily.com/releases/2003/10/031022062408.htm* (April 12, 2007).

21. [pg. 35] G. J. DeVries et al., "A Model System for Study of Sex Chromosome Effects on Sexually Dimorphic Neural and Behavioral Traits," *Journal of Neuroscience* 22, no. 20 (October 15, 2002): 9005–14.

22. [pg. 35] Hara Estroff Marano, "The New Sex Scorecard: Men and Women's Minds Really Do Work Differently—But Not on Everything." Posted July/August 2003. *Psychology Today: www.psychologytoday.com/articles/pto-20030624-000003.html* (April 12, 2007).

23. [pg. 36] DeVries, "A Model System for Study of Sex Chromosome Effects."

24. [pg. 36] *"New York Times columnist . . ."* Maureen Dowd, "X-celling Over Men," *New York Times*, March 20, 2005, section 4, page 13.

25. [pg. 36] Quoted in ibid.

26. [pg. 36] Moir and Jessel, *Brain Sex*, 11.

27. [pg. 37] Laura Carrel and Huntington F. Willard, "X-inactivation profile reveals extensive variability in X-linked gene expression in females," *Nature* 434, no. 7031 (March 17, 2005): 279–80.

28. [pg. 37] See Dowd, "X-celling Over Men."

29. [pg. 37] Genesis 1:26–28.

30. [pg. 37] Genesis 1:27–28.

31. [pg. 38] Svetlana Lutchmaya, Simon Baron-Cohen, and Peter Raggatt, "Foetal Testosterone and Eye Contact in 12-Month-Old Infants," *Infant Behavior and Development* 25 (2002): 327–35.

32. [pg. 38] Christina Hoff Sommers, *Who Stole Feminism?* (New York: Simon & Schuster, 1994), 73–74.

33. [pg. 38] Marano, "New Sex Scorecard."

34. [pg. 38] H. Hanlon, R. Thatcher, and M. Cline, "Gender Differences in the Development of EEG Coherence in Normal Children," *Developmental Neuropsychology* 16, no. 3 (1999): 479–506.

35. [pg. 38] Leonard Sax, *Why Gender Matters: What Parents and Teachers Need to Know about the Emerging Science of Sex Differences* (New York: Doubleday, 2005), 83.

36. [pg. 38] K. Dindia and M. Allen, "Sex Differences in Self-Disclosure: A Meta-Analysis," *Psychological Bulletin* 112 (1992): 106–24.

37. [pg. 39] Cited in Sax, *Why Gender Matters*, 83.

38. [pg. 39] Ibid.

39. [pg. 39] Quoted in Heubeck, "How Male and Female Brains Differ."

Chapter 2: Different as Night and Day

1. [pg. 44] "Brain Facts." *Brain Connection: www.brainconnection.com/ library/?main=explorehome/brain-facts* (April 12, 2007).

2. [pg. 44] Ibid.

3. [pg. 44] See Jeffrey M. Schwartz and Sharon Begley, *The Mind and the Brain* (New York: HarperCollins, 2003), 111.

4. [pg. 44] "What Is the World's Fastest Computer?" *How Stuff Works: http:// computer.howstuffworks.com/question54.htm* (April 12, 2007).

5. [pg. 46] Cited in Amanda Onion, "Scientists Find Sex Differences in Brain: Controversial Research Revealing Differences Between Men and Women." Posted January 19, 2005. *ABC News: http://abcnews.go.com/Technology/ Health/story?id=424260* (April 12, 2007).

6. [pg. 47] Michael Gurian, *What Could He Be Thinking? How a Man's Mind Really Works* (New York: St. Martin's, 2003), 82.

7. [pg. 49] Quoted in Joe Garofoli, "Femme Mentale: San Francisco Neuropsychiatrist Says Differences Between Women's and Men's Brains Are Very Real, and the Sooner We All Understand It, the Better." Posted August 6, 2006: A–1. *San Francisco Chronicle: http://sfgate.com/cgi-bin/ article.cgi?file=/c/a/2006/08/06/MNG3HKAMVO1.DTL* (April 12, 2007).

8. [pg. 51] P. H. Mehta and R. A. Josephs, "Testosterone Change after Losing Predicts the Decision to Compete Again," *Hormones and Behavior* 50, no. 5 (December 2006): 684–92. See also Anne Moir and David Jessel, *Brain Sex: The Real Difference Between Men and Women* (New York: Dell, 1992), 81.

9. [pg. 51] J. M. Dabbs Jr., D. de La Rue, and P. M. Williams, "Testosterone and Occupational Choice: Actors, Ministers, and Other Men," *Journal of Personality and Social Psychology* 59, no. 6 (December 1990): 1261–65.

10. [pg. 51] Moir and Jessel, *Brain Sex*, 95.

11. [pg. 51] Quoted in Steven E. Rhoads, "The Case Against Androgynous Marriage," *The American Enterprise: www.taemag.com/issues/ articleid.17048/article_detail.asp* (April 12, 2007).

12. [pg. 52] Cited in Marnia Robinson, "Your Brain on Sex," Posted June 25, 2005. *Reuniting: http://www.reuniting.info/science/sex_in_the_brain* (July 23, 2007).

13. [pg. 53] Gurian, *What Could He Be Thinking?* 45.

14. [pg. 53] Ibid., 44.

15. [pg. 53] Cited in Hara Estroff Marano, "The New Sex Scorecard: Men and Women's Minds Really Do Work Differently—But Not on Everything." Posted July/August 2003. *Psychology Today: www.psychologytoday.com/ articles/pto-20030624-000003.html* (April 12, 2007).

16. [pg. 53] Quoted in ibid.

17. [pg. 54] Gurian, *What Could He Be Thinking?* 13.

18. [pg. 54] Moir and Jessel, *Brain Sex*, 96.

19. [pg. 54] "Feeling Hormonal?" *IVillage: http://redbook.ivillage.com/ health/0,,9jr4v1b4–3,00.html* (April 12, 2007).

20. [pg. 56] quoted in Onion, "Scientists Find Sex Differences in Brain."

21. [pg. 57] Simon Baron-Cohen, *The Essential Difference: The Truth about the Male and Female Brain* (New York: Basic Books, 2003), 9.

22. [pg. 57] 1 Peter 3:7 NASB.

Chapter 3: Differences in How We Perceive Our World

1. [pg. 61] See Genesis 9:16: "Whenever the rainbow appears in the clouds, I will see it and remember the everlasting covenant between God and all living creatures of every kind on the earth."

2. [pg. 61] See Romans 1:20: "For since the creation of the world God's invisible qualities—his eternal power and divine nature—have been clearly seen, being understood from what has been made, so that men are without excuse."

3. [pg. 61] Quoted in Amanda Ripley, "Who Says a Woman Can't Be Einstein?" Posted Sunday, February 27, 2005. *Time Magazine: www.time.com/time/ printout/0,8816,1032332,00.html* (April 12, 2007).

4. [pg. 62] Cited in K. A. Jameson, S. M. Highnote, and L. M. Wasserman, "Richer Color Experience in Observers with Multiple Photopigment Opsin Genes," *Psychonomic Bulletin and Review* 8, no. 2 (June 2001): 244–61.

5. [pg. 62] Cited in Jennifer Connellan et al., "Sex Differences in Human Neonatal Social Perception," *Infant Behavior and Development* 23 (2001): 113–15.

6. [pg. 62] A. P. Bayliss, G. di Pellegrino, and S. P. Tipper, "Sex Differences in Eye Gaze and Symbolic Cueing of Attention," *Quarterly Journal of Experimental Psychology* 58, no. 4 (May 2005): 631–50.

7. [pg. 62] Cited in Svetlana Lutchmaya, Simon Baron-Cohen, and Peter Raggatt, "Foetal Testosterone and Eye Contact in 12-Month-Old Infants," *Infant Behavior and Development* 25 (2002): 327–35.

8. [pg. 63] Anne Moir and David Jessel, *Brain Sex: The Real Difference Between Men and Women* (New York: Dell, 1992), 18.
9. [pg. 63] Barbara and Allan Pease, *Why Men Don't Listen and Women Can't Read Maps: How We're Different and What to Do about It* (New York: Broadway Books, 2000), 21.
10. [pg. 63] Moir and Jessel, *Brain Sex*, 18.
11. [pg. 63] Pease, *Why Men Don't Listen*, 23.
12. [pg. 63] Tom Purcell, "Men and Women and Brains." Posted October 10, 2003. *Men's News Daily: http://mensnewsdaily.com/archive/p/purcell/03/purcell101003.htm* (April 13, 2007).
13. [pg. 64] J. K. Maner et al, "Sexually Selective Cognition: Beauty Captures the Mind of the Beholder," *Journal of Personality and Social Psychology* 85, no. 6 (December 2003): 1107–20. *Florida State University Department of Psychology: www.psy.fsu.edu/faculty/maner/sexually%20selective%20cognition.pdf* (April 12, 2007).
14. [pg. 64] Rick David, "The Latest Male/Female Brain Research (Shocking Revelations!)." *Merchant America San Diego: www.sandiego.merchantamerica.com/index.php?x=articles&periodical_key=3479* (April 12, 2007).
15. [pg. 64] Cited in Sandra F. Witelson, I. I. Glezer, and D. L. Kigar, "Women Have Greater Numerical Density of Neurons in Posterior Temporal Cortex," *Journal of Neuroscience* 15 (1995): 3418–28.
16. [pg. 65] Cited in Purcell, "Men and Women and Brains."
17. [pg. 65] K. Kansaku and S. Kitazawa, "Imaging Studies on Sex Differences in the Lateralization of Language," *Journal of Neuroscience Research* 41, no. 4 (December 2001): 333–37.
18. [pg. 65] Pease, *Why Men Don't Listen*, 30.
19. [pg. 65] Cited in J. Cassidy and K. Ditty, "Gender Differences among Newborns on a Transient Otoacoustic Emissions Test for Hearing," *Journal of Music Therapy* 38 (2001): 28–35. See also B. Cone-Wesson and G. Ramirez, "Hearing Sensitivity in Newborns Estimated from ABRs to Bone-Conducted Sounds," *Journal of the American Academy of Audiology* 8 (1997): 299–307.
20. [pg. 66] Pease, *Why Men Don't Listen*, 30.
21. [pg. 66] Moir and Jessel, *Brain Sex*, 17–18.
22. [pg. 66] Cited in "It's the Truth—Pain Hurts Women More than Men," *News-Medical: www.news-medical.net/?id=11498* (April 12, 2007).
23. [pg. 67] Cited in Pease, *Why Men Don't Listen*, 35.
24. [pg. 67] Cited in "It's the Truth—Pain Hurts Women More than Men."
25. [pg. 67] J. M. Reinisch, "Fetal Hormones, the Brain, and Human Sex Differences: A Heuristic, Integrative Review of the Recent Literature," *Archives of Sexual Behavior* 3, no. 1 (January 1974): 51–90.
26. [pg. 67] Cited in Pease, *Why Men Don't Listen*, 35.
27. [pg. 68] See I. Edward Alcamo, *Anatomy Coloring Workbook* (New York: Princeton Review, 2003), 136.

28. [pg. 68] Cited in L. Zhang and H. Q. Li, "Analysis of Taste Development in 62 Newborn Infants," *Chinese Journal of Pediatrics (Zhonghua Er Ke Za Zhi)* 44, no. 5 (May 2006): 350–55.

29. [pg. 68] P. Dalton, N. Doolittle, and P. A. Breslin, "Gender-Specific Induction of Enhanced Sensitivity to Odors," *Nature Neuroscience 5*, no. 3 (March 2002): 199–200.

30. [pg. 68] Cited in Tim Patterson, "Taste Bud Tales—Wine-Tasting Abilities of Women." *Find Articles: www.findarticles.com/p/articles/mi_m3488/ is_6_84/ai_103995707* (April 12, 2007).

31. [pg. 68] Cited in V. B. Duffy et al., "Taste Changes across Pregnancy," *Annals of the New York Academy of Sciences* 855 (November 30, 1998): 805–9.

32. [pg. 68] See Pease, *Why Men Don't Listen*, 37.

Chapter 4: Differences in How We Process Input from Our World

1. [pg. 70] Simon Baron-Cohen, "Is Autism an Extreme of the Male Condition?" Posted August 9, 2005. *The New York Times: www.iht.com/ articles/2005/08/08/opinion/edbaron.php* (April 12, 2007).

2. [pg. 70] Amanda Onion, "Scientists Find Sex Differences in Brain: Controversial Research Revealing Differences Between Men and Women." Posted January 19, 2005. *ABC News: http://abcnews.go.com/Technology/ Health/story?id=424260* (April 12, 2007).

3. [pg. 71] Simon Baron-Cohen, "They Just Can't Help It." Posted April 17, 2003. *The Guardian: http://www.guardian.co.uk/life/feature/ story/0,,937913,00.html* (July 25, 2007).

4. [pg. 71] Ibid.

5. [pg. 71] Adapted from Hara Estroff Marano, "The New Sex Scorecard: Men and Women's Minds Really Do Work Differently—But Not on Everything." Posted July/August 2003. *Psychology Today: www. psychologytoday.com/articles/pto-20030624-000003.html* (April 12, 2007).

6. [pg. 72] Cited in Barbara and Allan Pease, *Why Men Don't Listen and Women Can't Read Maps: How We're Different and What to Do about It* (New York: Broadway Books, 2000), 102.

7. [pg. 72] Anne Moir and David Jessel, *Brain Sex: The Real Difference Between Men and Women* (New York: Dell, 1992), 7.

8. [pg. 73] Quoted in Pease, *Why Men Don't Listen*, 109.

9. [pg. 73] Shelly E. Taylor et al., "Biobehavioral Responses to Stress in Females: Tend-and-Befriend, Not Fight-or-Flight," *Psychological Review* 107, no. 3 (2000): 411–29.

10. [pg. 73] Cited in Elizabeth Heubeck, "How Male and Female Brains Differ: Researchers Reveal Sex Differences in the Brain's Form and Function." Posted April 11, 2005. *WebMD Feature: www.medicinenet.com/script/ main/art.asp?articlekey=50512* (April 12, 2007).

11. [pg. 74] Helen S. Bateup et al., "Testosterone, Cortisol and Women's Competition," *Journal of Evolution and Human Behavior* 23, no. 3 (2002): 181–92. See also Helen Fisher, *The First Sex: The Natural Talents*

of *Women and How They Are Changing the World* (New York: Random House, 1999), 287; Anne Moir and Bill Moir, *Why Men Don't Iron: The Fascinating and Unalterable Differences between Men and Women* (New York: Citadel, 1999), 170–71.

12. [pg. 74] See Susan Golombok and Robyn Fivush, *Gender Development* (Cambridge: Cambridge Univ. Press, 1994), 164–65.

13. [pg. 74] See Fisher, *First Sex*, 29.

14. [pg. 74] See Steven E. Rhoads, *Taking Sex Differences Seriously* (San Francisco: Encounter Books, 2004), 140.

15. [pg. 74] See Kingsley R. Browne, "Sex and Temperament in Modern Society: A Darwinian View of the Glass Ceiling and the Gender Gap," *Arizona Law Review* 37, no. 3 (1995): 1024.

16. [pg. 74] See Golombok and Fivush, *Gender Development*, 164–65.

17. [pg. 74] See Eleanor E. Maccoby, *The Two Sexes: Growing Up Apart, Coming Together* (Cambridge, Mass.: Belknap, 1998), 39; see also Golombok and Fivush, *Gender Development*, 243.

18. [pg. 74] See Anemona Hartocollis, "Women Lawyers; Justice Is Blind. Also, a Lady." *The New York Times*, Sunday, April 1, 2001, section 4, page 3.

19. [pg. 74] Cited in ibid.

20. [pg. 74] Cited in ibid.

21. [pg. 75] Rhoads, *Taking Sex Differences Seriously*, 156.

22. [pg. 75] Cited in Browne, "Sex and Temperament in Modern Society," 1020. See also Katherine Blick Hoyenga and Kermit T. Hoyenga, *Gender-Related Differences: Origins and Outcomes* (Boston: Allyn and Bacon, 1993), 319.

23. [pg. 75] *"Other studies show the ..."* Moir, *Why Men Don't Iron*, 173.

24. [pg. 75] See " 'Sweet 16' Women Senators Talk Defense, Obama: 'GMA' Anchor Diane Sawyer Interviews Politicians on Being Women in Politics." Posted January 17, 2007. *ABC News: http://abcnews.go.com/GMA/ Politics/story?id=2801015* (April 12, 2007).

25. [pg. 75] Ibid., Senator Maria Cantwell (D-Washington).

26. [pg. 75] Ibid., Senator Mary Landrieu (D-Louisiana).

27. [pg. 75] Ibid., Senator Dianne Feinstein (D-California).

28. [pg. 75] Ibid., Senator Claire McCaskill (D-Missouri).

29. [pg. 75] Cited in Rhoads, *Taking Sex Differences Seriously*, 144.

30. [pg. 75] James M. Dabbs and Mary Godwin Dabbs, *Heroes, Rogues, and Lovers: Testosterone and Behavior* (New York: McGraw-Hill, 2000), 5, 13–14, 129–30, 138–39; see also Fisher, *First Sex*, 29.

31. [pg. 77] Quoted in Ronald Kotulak, "Gender and the Brain: New Evidence Shows How Hormones Wire the Minds of Men and Women to See the World Differently," *Chicago Tribune*, April 30, 2006, *http://www.rci. rutgers.edu/~shors/pdf/gender_brain_Apr30_2006.pdf* (August 1, 2007).

32. [pg. 78] Cited in Moir, *Why Men Don't Iron*, 86.

33. [pg. 79] Michael Gurian, *What Could He Be Thinking? How a Man's Mind Really Works* (New York: St. Martin's, 2003), 87.

34. [pg. 79] Cited in G. B. Hall et al., "Sex Differences in Functional Activation Patterns Revealed by Increased Emotion Processing Demands," *NeuroReport* 15, no. 2 (February 9, 2004): 219–23; see also J. D. Bremner et al., "Gender Differences in Cognitive and Neural Correlates of Remembrance of Emotional Words," *Psychopharmacology Bulletin* 35, no. 3 (Summer 2001): 55–78.

35. [pg. 79] Pease, *Why Men Don't Listen*, 135.

36. [pg. 80] See Onion, "Scientists Find Sex Differences in Brain."

37. [pg. 80] Shaunti and Jeff Feldhahn, *For Men Only: A Straightforward Guide to the Inner Lives of Women* (Sisters, Ore.: Multnomah, 2006), 54.

38. [pg. 81] See Bill and Pam Farrel, *Men Are Like Waffles — Women Are Like Spaghetti* (Eugene, Ore.: Harvest House, 2001).

39. [pg. 83] Minna Antrim, *Brainy Quote: http://www.brainyquote.com/quotes/quotes/m/minnaantri386699.html* (July 23, 2007).

40. [pg. 83] See C. Hutt, "Biological Bases of Psychological Sex Differences." Paper given to the European Society for Paediatric Endocrinology, Rotterdam, the Netherlands (June 1976).

41. [pg.83] Cited in Moir and Jessel, *Brain Sex*, 56.

42. [pg. 83] Ibid.

43. [pg. 84] Pease, *Why Men Don't Listen*, 19.

44. [pg. 84] 1 Kings 3:12; 4:29.

45. [pg. 85] Gilbert K. Chesterton, *Brainy Quote: http://www.brainyquote.com/quotes/quotes/g/gilbertkc156951.html* (July 23, 2007).

46. [pg. 85] Quoted in Elizabeth Weise, "Maybe We Are Different: New Book Argues Female Brain Wired to Nurture." Posted August 22, 2006. *USA Today: www.usatoday.com/tech/science/discoveries/2006-08-21-female-brain_x.htm* (April 12, 2007).

Chapter 5: Differences in How We Communicate with Our World

1. [pg. 87] Dave Stroder, "Potato Chip Fallout," *Marriage Partnership* (fall 2005). *Christianity Today: http://www.christianitytoday.com/mp/2005/003/5.50.html* (July 24, 2007). Used by permission.

2. [pg. 90] Anne Moir and David Jessel, *Brain Sex: The Real Difference Between Men and Women* (New York: Dell, 1992), 128.

3. [pg. 91] Cited in Barbara and Allan Pease, *Why Men Don't Listen and Women Can't Read Maps: How We're Different and What to Do about It* (New York: Broadway Books, 2000), 70.

4. [pg. 91] Cited in Michael Phillips et al., "Temporal Lobe Activation Demonstrates Sex-Based Differences During Passive Listening," *Radiology* 220, no. 1 (July 2001): 202–7.

5. [pg. 91] Cited in B. A. Shaywitz et al. "Sex Differences in the Functional Organization of the Brain for Language," *Nature* 373, no. 6515 (February 16, 1995): 607–9; see also A. M. Clements et al., "Sex Differences in Cerebral Laterality of Language and Visuospatial Processing," *Brain and Language* 98, no. 2 (August 2006): 150–58.

6. [pg. 91] See Doreen Kimura, "Sex Differences in the Brain: Men and Women Display Patterns of Behavioral and Cognitive Differences That Reflect Varying Hormonal Influences on Brain Development." Posted May 13, 2002. *Scientific American: http://sciam.com/print_version. cfm?articleID=00018E9D–879D–1D06–8E49809EC588EEDF* (April 12, 2007).

7. [pg. 92] Pease, *Why Men Don't Listen*, 80–81.

8. [pg. 92] Mark Liberman, "Sex-linked Lexical Budgets." *http://itre.cis.upenn. edu/~myl/languagelog/archives/003420.html* (August 1, 2007).

9. [pg. 92] Deborah James and Janice Drakich, "Understanding Gender Differences in Amount of Talk: A Critical Review of Research," in *Gender and Conversational Interaction*, ed. Deborah Tannen (New York: Oxford Univ. Press, 1993), 281–312.

10. [pg. 93] Cited in Matthias R. Mehl et al., "Are Women Really More Talkative Than Men?" *Science* 317 (July 2007): 82.

11. [pg. 93] Cited in Nancy Shute, "Chatty Cathy, Chatty Charlie: Surprise! A Study Finds Males Talk Just as much as Females," *US News and World Report: http://www.usnews.com/usnews/news/articles/070708/16talk.htm* (August 1, 2007).

12. [pg. 94] Moir and Jessel, *Brain Sex*, 136.

13. [pg. 94] See Michael Gurian, *What Could He Be Thinking? How a Man's Mind Really Works* (New York: St. Martin's, 2003), 92–93.

14. [pg. 94] Pease, *Why Men Don't Listen*, 78.

Chapter 6: Decoding Our Communication Differences

1. [pg. 97] Cited in Barbara and Allan Pease, *Why Men Don't Listen and Women Can't Read Maps: How We're Different and What to Do about It* (New York: Broadway Books, 2000), 197.

2. [pg. 97] Cited in Anne Moir and David Jessel, *Brain Sex: The Real Difference Between Men and Women* (New York: Dell, 1992), 135–36.

3. [pg. 97] Pease, *Why Men Don't Listen*, 83.

4. [pg. 97] Cited in Moir and Jessel, *Brain Sex*, 135–36.

5. [pg. 98] Willard F. Harley Jr., *His Needs, Her Needs: Building an Affair-Proof Marriage* (Grand Rapids: Revell, 2001), 69.

6. [pg. 98] Cited in Pease, *Why Men Don't Listen*, 94.

7. [pg. 99] Ibid.

8. [pg. 100] Moir and Jessel, *Brain Sex*, 128.

9. [pg. 100] Michael Gurian, *What Could He Be Thinking? How a Man's Mind Really Works* (New York: St. Martin's, 2003), 93.

10. [pg. 100] Moir and Jessel, *Brain Sex*, 136.

11. [pg. 101] Pease, *Why Men Don't Listen*, 136.

12. [pg. 102] Cited in Janice M. Steil, *Marital Equality: Its Relationship to the Well-Being of Husbands and Wives* (Thousand Oaks, Calif.: Sage, 1997), 214.

13. [pg. 102] Moir and Jessel, *Brain Sex*, 128.

14. [pg. 103] Gurian, *What Could He Be Thinking?* 93.

15. [pg. 104] Adapted from "What Women Say and What They MEAN." *Funny 2: http://www.funny2.com/women.htm* (August 1, 2007).

Chapter 7: Sex on the Brain

1. [pg. 112] "Marriage Enrichment: Conflict Resolution." *North Carolina State University: www.ces.ncsu.edu/depts/fcs/human/pubs/fcs-466-4.pdf* (April 12, 2007).

2. [pg. 112] Willard F. Harley Jr., *His Needs, Her Needs: Building an Affair-Proof Marriage* (Grand Rapids: Revell, 2001), 49.

3. [pg. 113] Cited in Barbara and Allan Pease, *Why Men Don't Listen and Women Can't Read Maps: How We're Different and What to Do about It* (New York: Broadway Books, 2000), 203–4.

4. [pg. 114] Ibid., 215.

5. [pg. 116] Cited in ibid., 220.

6. [pg.] Ibid.

7. [pg. 116] Cited in ibid., 226.

8. [pg. 117] Bruce J. Ellis and Donald Symons, "Sex Differences in Sexual Fantasy: An Evolutionary Psychological Approach," in *Human Nature: A Critical Reader*, ed. L. Betzig (New York: Oxford Univ. Press, 1997), 544.

9. [pg. 117] Pease, *Why Men Don't Listen*, 213.

10. [pg. 117] Cited in ibid., 194.

11. [pg. 118] Cited in Gary Langer, Cheryl Arnedt, and Dalia Sussman, "Primetime Live Poll: American Sex Survey: A Peek beneath the Sheets. Posted October 21, 2004. *ABC News: http://abcnews.go.com/Primetime/News/story/id=156921&page=1* (July 21, 2007).

12. [pg. 118] Cited in "Frequently Asked Sexual Questions," *Indiana University: http://www.indiana.edu/~kinsey/resources/FAQ.html* (August 1, 2007).

13. [pg. 118] Quoted in Anne Moir and David Jessel, *Brain Sex: The Real Difference Between Men and Women* (New York: Dell, 1992), 134.

14. [pg. 118] David C. Geary, *Male, Female: The Evolution of Human Sex Differences* (Washington, DC: American Psychological Association, 1998), 146.

15. [pg. 119] Cited in Shaunti and Jeff Feldhahn, *For Men Only: A Straightforward Guide to the Inner Lives of Women* (Sisters, Ore.: Multnomah, 2006), 30–31.

16. [pg. 119] Ibid., 130.

17. [pg. 119] Quoted in ibid., 128.

18. [pg. 119] Ibid., 126.

19. [pg. 119] Cited in Karlyn Bowman, "Poll Pourri: Love Sweet Love," *Women's Quarterly* (Winter), 13.

20. [pg. 120] Ross D. Parke and Douglas B. Sawin, "The Father's Role in Infancy: A Re-evaluation, *Family Coordinator* 25, no 4 (1976): 365–71.

21. [pg. 120] Adapted from Pease, *Why Men Don't Listen*, 212.

22. [pg. 121] Ibid., 211.

23. [pg. 121] Harley, *His Needs, Her Needs*, 43.

24. [pg. 121] Pease, *Why Men Don't Listen*, 212.

25. [pg. 121] See Harley, *His Needs, Her Needs*, 39.

26. [pg. 122] Ibid., 40.

27. [pg. 123] David M. Buss, *The Evolution of Desire* (New York: Basic Books, 1994), 71.

28. [pg. 123] John Stossel, "Lookism: The Ugly Truth about Beauty. Like It or Not, Looks Do Matter." Posted August 23, 2002. *ABC News: http://abcnews.go.com/2020/story?id=123853* (April 12, 2007).

29. [pg. 123] Quoted in Steven E. Rhoads, *Taking Sex Differences Seriously* (San Francisco: Encounter Books, 2004), 59.

30. [pg. 123] Pease, *Why Men Don't Listen*, 203.

31. [pg. 124] Harley, *His Needs, Her Needs*, 112.

32. [pg. 124] Ibid., 118 – 19.

33. [pg. 124] Ibid., 38.

34. [pg. 124] Rhoads, *Taking Sex Differences Seriously*, 110 – 11.

35. [pg. 125] See Linda J. Waite and Kara Joyner, "Emotional Satisfaction and Physical Pleasure in Sexual Unions: Time Horizon, Sexual Behavior, and Sexual Exclusivity," *Journal of Marriage and Family* 63, no. 1 (2001): 247 – 64.

36. [pg. 125] Cited in William R. Mattox Jr., "Marital Bliss," *American Enterprise* (May/June 1996), 45 – 46.

37. [pg. 125] Waite and Joyner, "Emotional Satisfaction and Physical Pleasure."

38. [pg. 125] Cited in Rhoads, *Taking Sex Differences Seriously*, 112.

39. [pg. 125] Cited in "Marital Sex — Beliefs about Marital Sexuality, Sexual Frequency, the Decline of Sexual Frequency Over Time, Sexual Practices and Preferences." *Marriage and Family Encyclopedia: http://family.jrank.org/pages/1109/Marital-Sex.html* (April 12, 2007).

40. [pg. 125] Cited in Rhoads, *Taking Sex Differences Seriously*, 112.

41. [pg. 125] See Gail Saltz, "Are You Keeping Up with Your Lover's Appetites?" *MSNBC: http://www.msnbc.msn.com/id/14301124/* (August 1, 2007).

42. [pg. 126] Adapted from Tim Gardner and Amy Gardner, "The Basics of Sex." Posted Fall 1999. *Christianity Today: www.christianitytoday.com/mp/9m3/9m3056.html* (April 12, 2007).

Chapter 8: Sex by God's Design

1. [pg. 128] See 1 Corinthians 7:2.

2. [pg. 128] See Hebrews 13:4.

3. [pg. 128] See Genesis 1:28a.

4. [pg. 128] See Deuteronomy 24:5; Proverbs 5:18 – 19; Song of Songs 4:10.

5. [pg. 129] Song of Songs 7:6 – 9 MSG.

6. [pg. 129] Genesis 1:31.

7. [pg. 129] See Song of Songs 5:1 – 16.

8. [pg. 129] See Hosea 1 – 3; Ephesians 5:21 – 33; 2 Corinthians 11:1 – 3; Revelation 19:6 – 9.

9. [pg. 129] Tim Gardner and Amy Gardner, "The Basics of Sex." Posted Fall 1999. *Christianity Today: www.christianitytoday.com/mp/9m3/9m3056. html* (April 12, 2007).

10. [pg. 129] Genesis 2:24 KJV.

11. [pg. 130] Janice Shaw Crouse, "Love Potion Number 'O.' " Posted January 25, 2006. *Concerned Women for America: www.cwfa.org/articledisplay. asp?id=9936&department=BLI&categoryid=dotcommentary* (April 12, 2007).

12. [pg. 130] R. A. Turner et al., "Preliminary Research on Plasma Oxytocin in Normal Cycling Women: Investigating Emotion and Interpersonal Distress," *Psychiatry* 62, no. 2 (Summer 1999): 97 – 113.

13. [pg. 130] "Hormone Involved in Reproduction May Have Role in the Maintenance of Relationships." Posted July 14, 1999. *UCSF News Office: http://pub.ucsf.edu/newsservices/releases/2004010721/* (April 12, 2007).

14. [pg. 131] Crouse, "Love Potion."

15. [pg. 131] Cited in Paula Rinehart, "A Union Like No Other," *Discipleship Journal* 27, no. 1 (January/February 2007): 43 – 47.

16. [pg. 131] See H. Fisher, A. Aron, and L. L. Brown, "Romantic Love: An fMRI Study of a Neural Mechanism for Mate Choice," *Journal of Comparative Neurology* 493, no. 1 (December 2005): 58 – 62.

17. [pg. 131] A. Bartels and S. Zeki, "The Neural Basis of Romantic Love," *NeuroReport* 11, no. 17 (November 27, 2000): 3829 – 934.

18. [pg. 132] Willard F. Harley Jr., *His Needs, Her Needs: Building an Affair-Proof Marriage* (Grand Rapids: Revell, 2001), 181.

19. [pg. 132] Ibid., 18.

20. [pg. 132] Ibid., 46.

21. [pg. 133] Cited in "Sexual Frequency," *Marriage and Family Encyclopedia: http://family.jrank.org/pages/1102/Marital-Sex-Sexual-Frequency.html* (July 22, 2007).

22. [pg. 133] See 1 Corinthians 7:4 MSG.

23. [pg. 133] Lorraine Pintus, "How to Be a Great Lover: Discover the Key to an Intimate Marriage," *Discipleship Journal* 27, no. 1 (January/February 2007): 49 – 57.

24. [pg. 133] Romans 12:10.

25. [pg. 133] Pintus, "How to Be a Great Lover," 51.

26. [pg. 134] Ibid.

27. [pg. 134] 1 Corinthians 7:3, 5.

28. [pg. 135] Genesis 2:24.

29. [pg. 135] Cited in Barbara and Allan Pease, *Why Men Don't Listen and Women Can't Read Maps: How We're Different and What to Do about It* (New York: Broadway Books, 2000), 224.

30. [pg. 135] Robert T. Michael et al., *Sex in America: A Definitive Survey* (Boston: Little, Brown, & Co., 1994), 1.

31. [pg. 135] See Edward O. Laumann et al., *The Social Organization of Sexuality: Sexual Practices in the United States* (Chicago: University of Chicago Press, 1994), 364, table 10.5.

32. [pg. 136] Michael et al., *Sex in America*, 131.
33. [pg. 136] Pintus, "How to Be a Great Lover," 51.
34. [pg. 137] Quoted in Michael Gurian, *What Could He Be Thinking? How a Man's Mind Really Works* (New York: St. Martin's, 2003), 137–38.
35. [pg. 137] Genesis 2:24.
36. [pg. 137] John 10:10 MSG.

Chapter 9: His Brain—Conquest; Her Brain—Nurture

1. [pg. 139] John Eldredge, *Wild at Heart: Discovering the Secret of a Man's Soul* (Nashville: Nelson, 2001), 4–5.
2. [pg. 140] Michael Gurian, *What Could He Be Thinking? How a Man's Mind Really Works* (New York: St. Martin's, 2003), 34.
3. [pg. 143] Ibid., 40–41.
4. [pg. 143] Quoted in Gurian, *What Could He Be Thinking?* 44.
5. [pg. 143] Anne Moir and David Jessel, *Brain Sex: The Real Difference Between Men and Women* (New York: Dell, 1992), 140.
6. [pg. 144] Cited in Theresa Crenshaw, *The Alchemy of Love and Lust* (New York: Putnam, 1996), 158, 184.
7. [pg. 145] Cited in Christina Hoff Sommers, *The War Against Boys* (New York: Simon & Schuster, 2000), 90.
8. [pg. 145] See Rob Stein, "Do Men Have Anger in Mind?" *Washington Post* (September 30, 2002).
9. [pg. 145] Cited in Steven E. Rhoads, *Taking Sex Differences Seriously* (San Francisco: Encounter Books, 2004), 135.
10. [pg.145] Cited in Anne Campbell, *A Mind of Her Own* (New York: Oxford Univ. Press, 2002), 105.
11. [pg. 145] Cited in Rhoads, *Taking Sex Differences Seriously*, 168.
12. [pg. 145] See A. D. Pelegrini and Jane C. Perlmutter, "Rough and Tumble Play on the Elementary School Yard," *Young Children* 43, no. 2 (1988): 14–47.
13. [pg. 145] See Eleanor E. Maccoby, *The Two Sexes: Growing Up Apart, Coming Together* (Cambridge, Mass.: Belknap, 1998), 102.
14. [pg. 146] Ibid., 62–64.
15. [pg. 146] Gurian, *What Could He Be Thinking?* 64.
16. [pg. 146] Cited in Kingsley R. Browne, *Biology at Work: Rethinking Sexual Equality* (New Brunswick, N.J.: Rutgers Univ. Press, 2002), 16.
17. [pg. 146] See Simon Baron-Cohen. Posted Winter 2005. *Phi Kappa Phi Forum: www.findarticles.com/p/articles/mi_qa4026/is_200501/ai_n13486678* (April 12, 2007).
18. [pg. 146] Eldredge, *Wild at Heart*, 9.
19. [pg. 147] Ibid.
20. [pg. 147] Gurian, *What Could He Be Thinking?* 46.
21. [pg. 147] Matthew 3:17.
22. [pg. 147] John 1:12–13.
23. [pg. 147] See Psalm 40:17; 18:19; Zephaniah 3:17.
24. [pg. 147] See Luke 15:10.
25. [pg. 147] See Deuteronomy 7:7; Philippians 1:8.

26. [pg. 148] See John 17:23.

27. [pg. 148] John 10:28.

28. [pg. 148] See Romans 7:24; Galatians 1:4; 2 Timothy 4:18; 2 Peter 2:9.

29. [pg. 148] Nehemiah 4:14.

30. [pg.148] Cited in Jerome H. Barkow, Leda Cosmides, and John Tooby, *The Adapted Mind: Evolutionary Psychology and the Generation of Culture* (New York: Oxford Univ. Press, 1992), 538.

31. [pg. 149] See David C. Geary, *Male, Female: The Evolution of Human Sex Differences* (Washington, DC: American Psychological Association, 1998), 219.

32. [pg. 149] Cited in Maccoby, *Two Sexes*, 39.

33. [pg. 149] Ibid., 37.

34. [pg. 149] Crenshaw, *Alchemy of Love and Lust*, 104.

35. [pg. 149] See Campbell, *Mind of Her Own*, 116 – 17.

36. [pg. 149] Helen Fisher, *The First Sex: The Natural Talents of Women and How They Are Changing the World* (New York: Random House, 1999), 29.

37. [pg. 149] See Geary, *Male, Female*, 250 – 51.

38. [pg. 149] See Campbell, *Mind of Her Own*, 55, 99.

39. [pg. 149] Crenshaw, *Alchemy of Love and Lust*, 184.

40. [pg. 149] Steven E. Rhoads, "The Case Against Androgynous Marriage," *The American Enterprise: www.taemag.com/issues/articleid.17048/article_detail.asp* (April 12, 2007).

41. [pg. 149] Cited in Sarah Blaffer Hrdy, *Mother Nature: A History of Mothers, Infants, and Natural Selection* (New York: Pantheon 1999), 137 – 39.

42. [pg. 149] Ibid., 137, 537 – 38.

43. [pg. 150] Cited in J. A. Russell, A. J. Douglas, and C. D. Ingram, "Brain preparations for maternity — adaptive changes in behavioral and neuroendocrine systems during pregnancy and lactation. An Overview," *Progress in Brain Research* 133 (2001): 1 – 38.

44. [pg. 150] Cited in Lynne E. Ford, *Women and Politics: The Pursuit of Equality* (Boston: Houghton-Mifflin, 2002), 285.

45. [pg. 150] Rhoads, *Taking Sex Differences Seriously*, 193.

46. [pg. 150] Myriam Khlat, Catherine Sermet, and Annick Le Pape, "Women's Health in Relation with Their Family and Work Roles: France in the early 1990s," *Social Science and Medicine* 50, no. 12 (June 2000): 1807 – 25.

47. [pg. 150] "Motherhood Today — A Tougher Job, Less Ably Done: As American Women See It." Posted May 9, 1997. *Pew Research Center: http://people-press.org/dataarchive/#1997* (April 12, 2007).

48. [pg. 150] Quoted in Rhoads, "Case Against Androgynous Marriage."

49. [pg. 150] Cited in Rhoads, *Taking Sex Differences Seriously*, 11.

50. [pg. 150] See Alan Wolfe, *Whose Keeper? Social Science and Moral Obligation* (Berkeley: University of California Press, 1991), 164.

51. [pg. 151] See Brad C. Gehrke, "Results of the 1997 AVMA Survey of U.S. Pet-Owning Households Regarding Use of Veterinary Services and

Expenditures," *American Veterinarian Medical Association* 211, no. 4 (1997): 417–18.

52. [pg. 151] Cited in Rhoads, *Taking Sex Differences Seriously*, 193.
53. [pg. 151] Cited in Rhoads, "Case Against Androgynous Marriage."
54. [pg. 151] Ibid.
55. [pg. 151] Gurian, *What Could He Be Thinking?* 62.
56. [pg. 152] Quoted in Rhoads, *Taking Sex Differences Seriously*, 262.
57. [pg. 152] Ibid., 63.
58. [pg. 152] Bernadette Gray-Little and Nancy Burks, "Power and Satisfaction in Marriage: A Review and Critique," *Psychological Bulletin* 93, no. 3 (1983): 513–38.
59. [pg. 152] Rhoads, *Taking Sex Differences Seriously*, 262.
60. [pg. 152] See Campbell, *Mind of Her Own*, 72, 110, 116.
61. [pg. 152] Rhoads, *Taking Sex Differences Seriously*, 152.
62. [pg. 152] Ibid., 153.
63. [pg. 153] Gray-Little and Burks, "Power and Satisfaction in Marriage," 513–38.
64. [pg. 153] Cited in Rhoads, *Taking Sex Differences Seriously*, 78.
65. [pg. 155] Gurian, *What Could He Be Thinking?* 63.
66. [pg. 155] Ibid.

Chapter 10: His Brain — Provision; Her Brain — Security

1. [pg. 158] See Michael Gurian, *What Could He Be Thinking? How a Man's Mind Really Works* (New York: St. Martin's, 2003), 147.
2. [pg. 159] See Linda Mealey, *Sex Differences: Developmental and Evolutionary Strategies* (San Diego: Academic Press, 2000), 272.
3. [pg. 159] See David M. Buss, *The Evolution of Desire* (New York: Basic Books, 1994), chapters 2–3.
4. [pg. 159] See Steven E. Rhoads, *Taking Sex Differences Seriously* (San Francisco: Encounter Books, 2004), 35.
5. [pg. 159] See ibid., 257.
6. [pg. 159] Anne Moir and David Jessel, *Brain Sex: The Real Difference Between Men and Women* (New York: Dell, 1992), 151.
7. [pg. 160] Ibid.
8. [pg. 161] See Gurian, *What Could He Be Thinking?* 147–48.
9. [pg. 161] Barbara and Allan Pease, *Why Men Don't Listen and Women Can't Read Maps: How We're Different and What to Do about It* (New York: Broadway Books, 2000), 137.
10. [pg. 161] Cited in Steven E. Rhoads, "The Case Against Androgynous Marriage," *The American Enterprise: www.taemag.com/issues/ articleid.17048/article_detail.asp* (April 12, 2007).
11. [pg. 161] Cited in Willard F. Harley Jr., *His Needs, Her Needs: Building an Affair-Proof Marriage* (Grand Rapids: Revell, 2001), 118.
12. [pg. 161] Cited in Rhoads, *Taking Sex Differences Seriously*, 61.
13. [pg. 161] Cited in Linda Thompson and Alexis J. Walker, "Gender in Families: Women and Men in Marriage, Work, and Parenthood," *Journal of Marriage and Family* 51 (1989): 853.

14. [pg. 162] Cited in Janice M. Steil, *Marital Equality: Its Relationship to the Well-Being of Husbands and Wives* (Thousand Oaks, Calif.: Sage, 1997), 50–55.

15. [pg. 162] Ibid.

16. [pg. 162] Ralph Gardner Jr., "Alpha Women, Beta Men: Wives are Increasingly Outearning Their Husbands, But Their New Financial Muscle Is Causing Havoc in the Home." Posted November 17, 2003. *New York Magazine: www.newyorkmetro.com/nymetro/news/features/n_9495/* (April 12, 2007).

17. [pg. 162] 1 Timothy 5:8.

18. [pg. 162] Rhoads, *Taking Sex Differences Seriously*, 253.

19. [pg. 162] Ibid., 256.

20. [pg. 163] Harley, *His Needs, Her Needs*, 124–25.

21. [pg. 163] Ibid., 126.

22. [pg. 163] Ibid., 130.

23. [pg. 164] Ibid., 124.

24. [pg. 165] Cited in "Motherhood Today—A Tougher Job, Less Ably Done: As American Women See It." Posted May 9, 1997. *Pew Research Center: http://people-press.org/dataarchive/#1997* (April 12, 2007).

25. [pg. 165] Ibid.

26. [pg. 165] Quoted in Jessica Anderson, "Myths of Motherhood." Posted August 29, 2005. *Concerned Women for America: http://www.cwfa.org/articledisplay.asp?id=8806&department=BLI&categoryid=family* (July 28, 2007).

27. [pg. 165] Quoted in ibid.

28. [pg. 165] Cited in "Motherhood Today—A Tougher Job, Less Ably Done."

29. [pg. 165] Suzanne Venker, *7 Myths of Working Mothers: Why Children and (Most) Careers Just Don't Mix* (Dallas: Spence, 2004). Quoted in "About This Book," *Spence Publishing Company: http://www.spencepublishing.com/books/index.cfm?action=Product&ProductID=79.*

30. [pg. 166] See Ric Edelman, "Should Both Parents Work? The Pros and Cons." Posted 2002. *About.com: http://homeparents.about.com/cs/familyfinances/a/bothwork.htm.* (April 12, 2007).

31. [pg. 166] See "Motherhood Today—A Tougher Job, Less Ably Done."

32. [pg. 166] Rhoads, *Taking Sex Differences Seriously*, 259.

33. [pg. 167] Harley, *His Needs, Her Needs*, 125.

34. [pg. 167] Cited in Shaunti and Jeff Feldhahn, *For Men Only: A Straightforward Guide to the Inner Lives of Women* (Sisters, Ore.: Multnomah, 2006), 77.

35. [pg. 168] Harley, *His Needs, Her Needs*, 95.

36. [pg. 170] See Rhoads, "Case Against Androgynous Marriage."

37. [pg. 170] Harley, *His Needs, Her Needs*, 192.

38. [pg. 170] Ibid., 135.

39. [pg. 170] Ibid., 136.

40. [pg. 170] Cited in Rhoads, "Case Against Androgynous Marriage"; see also Philip Blumstein and Pepper Schwartz, *American Couples: Money, Work, and Sex* (New York: Morrow, 1983).

41. [pg. 171] "Modern Marriage: 'I Like Hugs. I Like Kisses. But What I Really Love Is Help with the Dishes.'" Posted July 18, 2007. *Pew Research Center: http://pewresearch.org/pubs/542/modern-marriage* (July 27, 2007).

42. [pg. 171] Catherine Hakim, *Work-Lifestyle Choices in the Twenty-First Century* (New York: Oxford Univ. Press, 2000), 100.

Chapter 11: His Brain — Respect; Her Brain — Love

1. [pg. 173] Michael Gurian, *What Could He Be Thinking? How a Man's Mind Really Works* (New York: St. Martin's, 2003), 126.

2. [pg. 173] Ibid.

3. [pg. 174] Willard F. Harley Jr., *His Needs, Her Needs: Building an Affair-Proof Marriage* (Grand Rapids: Revell, 2001), 156.

4. [pg. 175] Emerson Eggerichs, *Love and Respect: The Love She Most Desires; The Respect He Desperately Needs* (Nashville: Integrity, 2004), 16.

5. [pg. 175] Shaunti Feldhahn, *For Women Only: What You Need to Know about the Inner Lives of Men* (Sisters, Ore.: Multnomah, 2004), 25.

6. [pg. 176] Ibid., 48 – 49.

7. [pg. 176] Proverbs 12:4.

8. [pg. 176] Colossians 3:19.

9. [pg. 176] Harley, *His Needs, Her Needs*, 38, 44 – 46.

10. [pg. 177] Philippians 2:3 – 7.

11. [pg. 177] James 3:16.

12. [pg. 178] Ephesians 5:21 RSV.

13. [pg. 178] Ephesians 5:25.

14. [pg. 178] Ephesians 5:28 – 30.

15. [pg. 178] Colossians 3:19.

16. [pg. 179] See Mark 9:50.

17. [pg. 179] See Romans 12:10.

18. [pg. 179] See 1 Thessalonians 4:18.

19. [pg. 179] See 1 Thessalonians 5:11.

20. [pg. 179] See Galatians 5:13.

21. [pg. 179] See Romans 12:10.

22. [pg. 179] See Romans 16:16.

23. [pg. 179] See Galatians 5:26.

24. [pg. 179] See Colossians 3:13.

25. [pg. 179] See Ephesians 4:2.

26. [pg. 179] See ibid.

27. [pg. 179] Ephesians 5:33.

28. [pg. 180] Feldhahn, *For Women Only*, 22.

29. [pg. 181] Ephesians 5:33.

30. [pg. 182] Avery Cardinal Dulles, "Love, the Pope, and C. S. Lewis," *First Things* (January 2007): 20 – 24. *First Things: www.firstthings.com/article. php3?id_article=5393* (April 12, 2007).
31. [pg. 183] Titus 2:4 NASB.
32. [pg. 183] See Feldhahn, *For Women Only*, 28 – 48.
33. [pg. 183] Ibid., 32 – 33.
34. [pg. 183] See Shaunti and Jeff Feldhahn, *For Men Only: A Straightforward Guide to the Inner Lives of Women* (Sisters, Ore.: Multnomah, 2006), 15 – 17.
35. [pg. 183] John Eldredge and Stasi Eldredge, *Captivating: Unveiling the Mystery of a Woman's Soul* (Nashville: Nelson, 2005), 112.
36. [pg. 184] 1 Peter 3:7; see also 1 Timothy 3:11 and 1 Peter 2:17.
37. [pg. 184] Titus 2:4.

Chapter 12:Created to Be One by God's Design

1. [pg. 187] Genesis 2:7.
2. [pg. 187] See Brown-Driver-Briggs Hebrew Lexicon. *Blue Letter Bible: www. blueletterbible.org/cgi-bin.blb/strongs.pl?hr=http%3A%2F%2Fwww. eliyah.com%2Flexicon.html&icon=http%3A%2F%2Fwww.eliyah. com%2Fbackto. gif&bgcolor=FFFFFF&textcolor=000000&linkcolor=0000FF &vlinkcolor=A000FF&language=H&strongs=3335* (April 12, 2007).
3. [pg. 187] Genesis 2:22.
4. [pg. 188] See Brown-Driver-Briggs Hebrew Lexicon. *Blue Letter Bible.*
5. [pg. 188] Genesis 1:4, 10, 12, 18, 21, 25.
6. [pg. 188] Genesis 2:18.
7. [pg. 189] R. David Freedman, "Woman Power Equal to Man," *Biblical Archaeology Review* 9 (January/February 1983). *University of Chicago: http://home.uchicago.edu/~spackman/powerequaltoman.pdf* (April 12, 2007).
8. [pg. 190] Footnotes to Genesis 2:18. *The Net Bible: http://net.bible.org/ verse.php?book=Gen&chapter=2&verse=18.* Used by permission of www. bible.org (April 12, 2007). See also M. L. Rosenzweig, "A Helper Equal to Him," *Judaism* 139 (1986): 277 – 80.
9. [pg. 190] Samuel Terrien, *Till the Heart Sings: A Biblical Theology of Manhood and Womanhood* (Philadelphia: Fortress, 1985), 9.
10. [pg. 191] Genesis 2:20.
11. [pg. 191] Genesis 2:21 – 22.
12. [pg. 191] Genesis 2:18.
13. [pg. 191] Genesis 2:22.
14. [pg. 192] Genesis 2:23.
15. [pg. 192] Ibid.
16. [pg. 193] Genesis 2:24.
17. [pg. 195] Ecclesiastes 4:9 – 12.

Chapter 13: Cherish, Honor, Nurture by God's Design

1. [pg. 197] 1 Peter 3:7.
2. [pg. 197] 1 Peter 3:7 NASB.
3. [pg. 198] *Quote World: http://www.quoteworld.org/quotes/725* (July 28, 2007).
4. [pg. 198] 1 Peter 3:7.
5. [pg. 198] See "A Concise Dictionary of the Words in the Greek New Testament," in James Strong, *Strong's Exhaustive Concordance of the Bible* (Nashville: Abingdon, 1986), 18.
6. [pg. 199] Ephesians 5:29.
7. [pg. 200] Romans 15:14.
8. [pg. 200] Colossians 3:16.
9. [pg. 200] Ephesians 5:19.
10. [pg. 200] See Deuteronomy 6:6–9.
11. [pg. 200] See Strong, "A Concise Dictionary," 46.
12. [pg. 201] Psalm 91:4.
13. [pg. 201] 1 Peter 3:7 MSG.
14. [pg. 202] This poem combines words from two sources: J. Allan Petersen, *The Myth of the Greener Grass*, revised edition (Wheaton, Ill.: Tyndale, 1991), 183; "Keep the Box Full," bulletin insert published by Better Families, February 1998. Used by permission.
15. [pg. 203] *Brainy Quote: www.brainyquote.com/quotes/quotes/a/alexvanhal216209.html* (April 12, 2007).
16. [pg. 204] John Gray, *Men Are from Mars, Women Are from Venus* (New York: HarperCollins, 1992), 14.
17. [pg. 204] Jeremiah 17:9.
18. [pg. 204] Ezekiel 36:26–28.

Scripture Index

Subject Index

Alternative Medicine

The Christian Handbook, Updated and Expanded

*Dónal O'Mathúna, PhD,
and Walt Larimore, MD*

The most complete resource of its kind

- Herbal remedies, dietary supplements, and alternative therapies and their specific uses
- Which ones really work (and which ones don't) and what to watch out for
- And much, much more

Alternative Medicine is the first comprehensive guidebook to nontraditional medicine written from a distinctively Christian perspective. Keeping pace with the latest developments and research in alternative medicine, this thoroughly revised edition combines the most current information with an easy-to-use format.

Also includes

- Two alphabetical reference sections:
    - Alternative therapies
    - Herbal remedies, vitamins, and dietary supplements
- A description of each therapy and remedy, an analysis of claims, results of actual studies, cautions, recommendations, and further resources

Softcover 0-310-26999-7

Pick up a copy today at your favorite bookstore!

Bryson City Series

Walt Larimore, MD

Told with winsome humor and deep affection, Dr. Walt Larimore's engaging stories serve up a rich fare of Smoky Mountain personalities, highland wisdom, and all the tears, laughter, tenderness, courage, and adventures (and even misadventures) of small-town life. Lit with love, humor, glowing faith, and the warmth of family and friendship, and tempered with the bright and dark realities of country medicine, these books will capture your imagination and warm your heart. Guaranteed!

Bryson City Tales

Softcover 0-310-25670-4

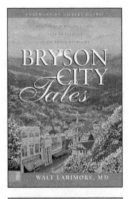

Bryson City Seasons

Softcover 0-310-25672-0

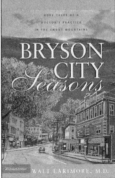

Bryson City Secrets

Hardcover, Jacketed 0-310-26633-5
Softcover 0-310-26634-3

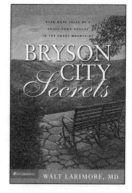

Best of Bryson City

Synopsis: Telling selected true stories from his books *Bryson City Tales* and *Bryson City Secrets*, Walt Larimore shares the heart, the humor, and the humility of a raw young doctor in his first days in a little town in the Smoky Mountains.

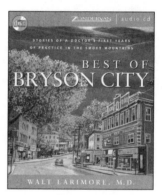

Audio CD, Abridged 0-310-25505-8
Audio Download, Unabridged 0-310-261406

Pick up a copy today at your favorite bookstore!

We want to hear from you. Please send your comments about this
book to us in care of zreview@zondervan.com. Thank you.

ZONDERVAN.com/
AUTHORTRACKER
follow your favorite authors